THE NEW YORK PUBLIC LIBRARY AMAZING WOMEN IN AMERICAN HISTORY
A Book of Answers for Kids

Sue Heinemann

A Stonesong Press Book

John Wiley & Sons, Inc.
New York • Chichester • Weinheim • Brisbane • Singapore • Toronto

Copyright ©1998 by The New York Public Library and The Stonesong Press, Inc.
Published by John Wiley & Sons, Inc.

Library of Congress Cataloging-in-Publication Data

Heinemann, Sue.
    The New York Public Library amazing women in American history: a book of answers for kids / Sue Heinemann.
       p.   cm. — (New York Public Library answer books for kids series)
    "A Stonesong Press book."
    Includes index.
    Summary: Consists of short answers to questions about the roles and achievements of women in America from prehistory to the end of the twentieth century.
    ISBN 0-471-19216-3 (alk. paper)
    1. Women—United States—History—Juvenile literature.
2. Questions and answers—Juvenile literature. [1. Women—History—Miscellanea.
2. Women—Social conditions—Miscellanea. 3. Women's rights—Miscellanea.
4. Women—Biography. 5. Questions and answers.] I. Title. II. Series.
HQ1410.H43   1998
973' .082—dc21   97-18465

Printed in the United States of America

10 9 8 7 6 5 4 3 2 1

CONTENTS

INTRODUCTION

What did women do during the Revolutionary War? When did the U.S. movement for women's rights begin? Who were Susan B. Anthony, Harriet Tubman, and Eleanor Roosevelt?

There are hundreds of questions to ask about the history of women in the United States, and thousands of amazing women to learn about. With *The New York Public Library Amazing Women in American History*, you can quickly find answers to many of the most important questions and meet some of the incredible women who helped shape U.S. history.

The New York Public Library Amazing Women in American History is only an introduction to the many contributions women have made to our history. It would take a whole library of books to tell the full story! But the information in this book offers a good start for an exciting exploration of the many different ways women have enriched our history — in politics, education, religion, the arts, and other areas.

Let the questions and answers in this book spark your curiosity and suggest new questions and new subjects to investigate. Then do your own research. Check out the bibliography and the suggested reading list for additional sources of information. Also take a trip to the library. The New York Public Library and other libraries all over the country have both books and computers filled with amazing facts that you can discover on your own. Ask the librarian if you need some help locating the information you want. We hope that this book will lead you on your own exciting investigation of women's history and will encourage you to use your local library.

THE FIRST AMERICAN WOMEN (PREHISTORIC TIMES – 1760)

Who were the first women in America? ◆ What was life like for early Native American women? ◆ How important were women in Native American societies? ◆ Were any women chiefs? ◆ When did European women arrive in America? Where did the first women come from in England? ◆ Who were the first permanent English women settlers? ◆ What is the real story of Pocahontas? ◆ Were there any African women in Jamestown? ◆ Were any white women slaves? ◆ Was it easy for white women to find husbands in America? ◆ When did the English women arrive? What kinds of work did women settlers do? ◆ Did any women run

Who were the first women in America?

Archaeologists have discovered that people lived in America at least 12,000 to 15,000 years ago, and perhaps even 40,000 years ago. These people probably came from Siberia, traveling across a bridge of frozen land that once existed between Russia and Alaska. Over thousands of years, their descendants moved south and east, settling throughout the Americas and giving birth to the many different Native American peoples.

What was life like for early Native American women?

Not much is known about the first women, who probably moved with their families from place to place in search of food. As Native Americans settled in different areas, women helped farm the land, from preparing the soil to harvesting corn and other vegetables. To store the food and carry water, they created beautiful baskets and pottery with artistic patterns. Some women even designed and built their homes, such as the **tipis** made by Plains women.

How important were women in Native American societies?

Indian creation myths suggest that women have always had important roles in Native American cultures. Many societies were **matrilineal**, tracing their ancestry

Spear points from 10,000 to 11,000 years ago have been discovered in present-day Colorado and New Mexico, and there are signs of equally old wood-post dwellings in the Shenandoah Valley in Virginia.

This Edward Curtis photograph (c.1920) shows Native American Hopi women preparing cornmeal as their ancestors have done for thousands of years.

through women called **clan mothers**. In some groups the right to hold office was inherited from the mother. Among the Iroquois and Cherokee, women sat on decision-making councils, and clan mothers nominated chiefs and could overthrow them.

Were any women chiefs?

When the first Europeans arrived in America, they encountered several female rulers. One was the **cacica** (chief) of Cutifachiqui, in what is now Georgia. Around 1540 she greeted the Spanish explorer Hernando de Soto and gave him pearls and other gifts. De Soto then turned on her, took her captive, and used her as a guide as he marched north. But the cacica was clever and escaped after two weeks. She took with her some of the most valuable pearls.

When did European women arrive in America?

The first European woman in America was Francesca Hinestrosa of Spain. She joined her husband on de Soto's expedition from Florida through Georgia and the Carolinas and then west, across the Appalachians toward the Mississippi. She was killed in an attack by Chickasaw warriors in 1541. Later, in 1565, Spanish women helped settle Saint Augustine in Florida. There, in 1566, Señora Argüelles gave birth to a boy, the first known child of European parents in what is now the United States.

When did the first women come from England?

In 1587 about 120 British colonists, including 17 women and several children, settled on Roanoke Island in what was then called Virginia (now North Carolina). There Virginia Dare, the first American child of English parents, was born on August 18, 1587. What happened to her, as well as the rest of the colonists, is a mystery. Nine days after her birth, her grandfather, the colony's governor, set sail for England. When he returned three years later, there was no one on the island. Some people believe that the settlers died in an Indian attack; others say that they moved to the mainland and intermarried with Native Americans there.

Who were the first permanent English women settlers?

In 1608, a year after the founding of the Jamestown settlement in Virginia, Anne Forrest joined her husband there. With her was her 13-year-old maid, Anne Buras. In the next

One of the first European maps of the Southwest was based on a drawing made in the dirt in 1542 by a Wichita woman known as Big Eyes.

The Goddess Stories

In several different Native American creation stories, the world is brought into existence by a woman. The Keres Indians and the Navajo speak of Thinking Woman, also called Spider Woman, who "thought the earth, the sky, the galaxy, and all that is into being," in the words of writer Paula Gunn Allen. The Iroquois tell of Sky Woman, who fell through the sky from another world and eventually found herself on the back of a turtle. There, in the layer of earth covering the turtle's back, she planted the tree of life.

*In the early 1600s
Iroquois women
stopped all love-
making until men
gave them the
right to decide
between war and
peace. It didn't
take the men long
to agree.*

year about 120 more women arrived in Jamestown, but many died from starvation, illness, or Indian attacks.

What is the real story of Pocahontas?

Pocahontas was the daughter of Powhatan, the most powerful chief in the area the English called Virginia. She was about 12 or 13 in 1607, when the Jamestown settlement was founded. That same year she supposedly begged her father not to kill Captain John Smith, a Jamestown leader, after he was captured as a presumed enemy. Six years later Pocahontas was taken hostage by the British to give them more power in negotiations with Powhatan. Brought to Jamestown, she converted to Christianity and married the colonist John Rolfe in 1614, possibly to help keep peace between her people and the British. In 1617 Pocahontas (now called Rebecca) died in England, where she had been introduced to the queen.

A Native American village near Jamestown, as depicted by an English settler, shows carefully tended crops and buildings. Native American women were often in charge of most of the farming for their community.

Were there any African women in Jamestown?

In 1619 the first Africans, including three women, were brought to British America. They arrived in Jamestown as **indentured servants**, who had to work for their "masters" for a set number of years but then gained their freedom. Within the next few decades, however, more and more Africans were forced into slavery. In Spanish America (Florida, Mexico, Cuba, and other lands held by the Spanish), slavery began much earlier, with some of the first settlements.

Were any white women slaves?

White women were not sold as slaves, but many poor English women agreed to work for five to seven years as indentured servants in return for payment for their trip to America. They helped with farmwork and in the household. Afterward they usually married.

Was it easy for white women to find husbands in America?

At first, many more men came to America than women, and wives were much in demand. Some women were even imported as wives. In 1620 about ninety British women landed in Jamestown to be "sold" as wives. Men rushed to pay the 120 pounds of tobacco (about $80) that the shipowners charged for transporting a wife.

When did the Pilgrim women arrive?

The *Mayflower,* with eighteen women and eleven girls among its passengers, landed at Plymouth Rock in Massachusetts in 1620. Mary Chilton was the first woman to step ashore. Many of the women died during the first, bitterly cold winter, but all the girls survived.

What kinds of work did women settlers do?

In addition to helping with the farming, women cooked and baked and preserved food for the winter. They made their family's clothes by spinning, weaving, and stitching by hand. They also made candles, soap, and other household supplies. Women served as **midwives**, assisting

Colonial women cooked their families' meals over an open fire in a huge fireplace. For baking, they used a tightly covered cast-iron kettle, known as a Dutch oven, which was hooked onto a crane and swung over the fire.

mothers when they gave birth to their children. Women also took care of the children.

Did any women run their own farms or businesses?

Although married women could not own property in the British colonies, they helped keep the farm and family businesses going. They might shoe horses, operate a printing press, or look after a store. The wives of traders, especially in the Dutch colony of New Amsterdam (now New York), often took charge of farms or businesses when their husbands were away. In addition, widows and unmarried women, who could own property, sometimes managed estates.

Did any women serve in colonial governments?

Women settlers generally had no role in government. One exception was Lady Deborah Moody of England, who in 1643 became the first woman to head a colonial settlement. Desiring religious freedom, she and her followers started a community in what is now Brooklyn, New York. Lady Moody received a charter from the Dutch for the town and helped set up its government.

Were early women settlers religious?

Many early immigrants, such as the **Puritans** in Massachusetts, came to America in order to practice their religion freely. Puritan ministers often praised women for

The Woman Who Saved Maryland

In 1638 Margaret Brent received a land grant in Maryland and set up a successful plantation with her sister Mary. Margaret Brent often went to court to carry out legal transactions for herself and others. In 1647, when Lord Calvert, the governor of Maryland, was dying, he put her in charge of his estate. At the time the governor's soldiers were about to rebel because they had not been paid. Brent calmed them and found a way to pay them, saving Maryland from a revolt. The Maryland assembly later praised her efforts. But when she asked for two votes in the assembly because she owned her property and was also in charge of Lord Calvert's estate, the assembly turned her down.

An Early Poet

Anne Bradstreet was 18 when she came to Massachusetts from England in 1630. While raising eight children and doing all the work of a female settler, she wrote her poems. In 1650, without her consent, her brother-in-law took some of her poems to London and had them published. This volume, *The Tenth Muse Lately Sprung Up in America*, was the first book published by an American woman. Another book of her poems was published after her death. In one poem, to her husband, she wrote: "If ever two were one then surely we. / If ever man were loved by wife, then thee."

their devotion to God and their religious obedience. The Puritans did not, however, believe that these good women should speak in church or preach in any way. In contrast, the **Quakers**, who settled mostly in Pennsylvania, allowed women to be ministers.

Did any Puritan women try to preach?

At meetings in her home in Boston, Anne Hutchinson claimed that many of the Puritan preachers were wrong and that it was not good deeds but God's grace that would save people. When some influential men became her followers, the church authorities grew alarmed. By emphasizing each person's direct link to God, she threatened the power of the clergy. In 1637–38 she was put on trial for going against the ministers, found guilty, and banished from the Massachusetts colony. She went to Rhode Island and later to New Netherland (now New York), where she was killed by Indians.

Did other women stand up for their religious beliefs?

Almost all the early women who made a strong stand for religious freedom were Quakers. Some Quaker women became missionaries and traveled outside the Quaker colony of Pennsylvania to convert others to their faith. In Massachusetts, where only the Puritan faith was permitted, several Quaker women missionaries were put in prison or

Quaker women held their own business meetings; one of their main duties was to determine if a couple was ready for marriage.

Anne Hutchinson spoke and taught about Puritan beliefs, which did not please some of the Puritan ministers, who were all male. She was banished from the Massachusetts colony in 1638. An early 20th century painting by noted illustrator Howard Pyle depicts her preaching.

publicly whipped. Mary Dyer, banned from Boston for supporting Anne Hutchinson, became a Quaker and in 1657 returned to preach her beliefs. When Massachusetts passed a law calling for the death of anyone teaching Quaker ideas, Dyer did not back down. In 1659 she was arrested, marched through the streets to be hanged, but released at the last minute and sent to Rhode Island. Six months later she was back, protesting the unjust law and insisting on religious freedom. This time she was hanged. Today there is a statue in her honor in Boston.

Were there Catholic women in colonial America?

In the 1600s English Catholics such as Margaret Brent settled in Maryland, which was set up as a safe colony for Catholics. In the French colonies in Canada and the Spanish colonies in Florida and the Southwest, a number of Native American women were converted to Catholicism by missionaries, who were mostly men at that time. Katerí Tekakwitha, a Mohawk woman, was stoned by her people when she converted in 1676. Tekakwitha became a nun noted for her strong faith. After she died, people who visited her tomb reported miraculous cures. In 1980 the Catholic Church beatified her, a major step toward her being named a saint.

When Katerí Tekakwitha died in 1680, at age 24, it was said that the smallpox scars on her face suddenly disappeared, making her beautiful.

What was the religion of African women in America?

The African women captured and brought to America held many different religious beliefs. Some were followers of the Islamic religion; others came from West African religious traditions in which women priests and healers played important roles. It was difficult, however, to practice their religions in America. Many African women eventually converted to Christianity, but they often found ways to continue to serve as healers and prophets.

What was life like for black women held in slavery?

Many female slaves, especially in the South, were forced to work all day in the fields, planting, tending, and harvesting rice, tobacco, cotton, and other crops. If they did not work hard enough, they were whipped. Some women served as "house slaves," carrying water, washing clothes, cleaning, cooking, and the like. After they finished the day's work for the slave owners, they still had to do their own washing, cleaning, and cooking.

Slave owners expected female slaves to bear lots of children, who could be taken away and sold to other slave owners, never to be seen again. Female slaves could also be raped, given husbands of the master's choosing, or sold to another master.

Did any female slaves fight for their freedom in colonial times?

In 1655 Elizabeth Key, the daughter of a white man and an African woman held in slavery, sued for her freedom. She won because under Virginia law at the time, a child inherited the father's status. The law, however, was quickly changed. As slavery became more rigidly enforced in the 1660s, some African American women risked their lives by joining slave revolts.

How long did slavery last?

Many black women in colonial America were slaves for their entire lives. Although slavery began to be abolished in some northern states in the late 1770s, during the Revolutionary War, it continued in the South until the end of the Civil War in 1865.

Were any Native American women slaves?

Most slaves were of African descent, but a few women captured in Native American uprisings were sold into slavery in the Caribbean. Other women, captured in wars between Native American tribes, were used as slaves by their conquerors and sometimes sold to European soldiers and traders. In the Southwest, some Pueblo women were forced to work for the Spanish.

What happened to white women captured by Native Americans?

The experiences of the white women who were captured in Indian raids varied. Some were later killed; some

Two Sides of a Story

Mary Rowlandson was taken from her Massachusetts home in 1676 by the Narragansetts and had to march about 150 miles. A devout Puritan, she hated the Indian way of life, saw her captors as "vile savages," and especially disliked Weetamoo, the female leader she had to serve. Rowlandson negotiated a ransom for her release and later wrote a popular book about her three-month experience.

Although we do not know what Weetamoo felt about Mary Rowlandson, we do know that Weetamoo was an important **sachem**, or leader, who was strongly against giving more land or rights to the English settlers. At one point she had 300 warriors under her command. After she drowned in 1676 during the Native American uprising called King Philip's War, the Puritans put her head on display, an act that shows how powerful they thought she was.

escaped; some became servants; and some became members of their captors' families. A few white women chose to remain with their Indian captors even when offered a chance to return to white civilization. The best-known example was Mary Jemison, who was adopted by the Seneca in 1758, at age 14. Later, she recalled how the Seneca women had accepted her as a true sister, as if she "had been born of the same mother."

Were there many Native American women leaders?

We do not know how many Native American women were leaders in the colonial period, but the names of a few appear in white settlers' accounts. At least two sachems fought against the English in the mid-1670s in King Philip's War: Weetamoo and Magnus. Another sachem, Awashonks, decided that to protect her people during King Philip's War she must honor an earlier agreement not to fight the English, so she helped the settlers.

A very important woman leader was Nanye-hi, also known as Nancy Ward. In 1755, after her husband was killed in battle, she took charge and led the Cherokees to a victory over Creek warriors. Honored by the Cherokees as "Beloved Woman," she headed an advisory group of women elders and was a member of the governing council of chiefs. She helped negotiate peace agreements with white settlers. Like many Native American chiefs, she was surprised that no white women were allowed to negotiate.

Were there any European American women leaders in the late 1600s to early 1700s?

Not many white women were leaders at this time. A rare exception was María Betancour, who in 1731 led a group of settlers from the Canary Islands, off the coast of Spain, to Texas, where she helped establish the town of San Antonio.

Did women in the 1700s have other important roles?

There were women blacksmiths, butchers, shopkeepers, traders, inventors, and shipbuilders in the 1700s. A number of women published newspapers, including Elizabeth Timothy, who edited the *South-Carolina*

In Virginia "Queen Anne" (as the English called her) protested against colonial demands for land and money from the Pamunkeys and in 1715 argued for her people's rights before the Virginia assembly.

In 1744 Eliza Lucas, who ran her father's three plantations in South Carolina, successfully grew a crop of indigo, a plant used to make a blue dye. She urged other planters to grow indigo, and it soon became the colony's leading export.

The Salem Witchhunt

In 1692 in Salem, Massachusetts, a group of 9- to 11-year-old girls were fascinated by stories told by Tituba, a slave, and began playing with the idea of magic. They pretended to have fits and then claimed they were the victims of spells cast by witches in the town. Because, at the time, people believed in witches as representations of the Devil, these were serious charges and the suspected witches were arrested. The girls' "fits" continued, and more and more people were arrested. At the trials the male judges accepted the girls' frantic screams as proof of witchcraft. Many of those accused "confessed" and asked to be forgiven. Those who did not, however, were sentenced to die. In the end 14 women, including the highly respected Rebecca Nurse, and 6 men were killed. All were later shown to be innocent.

In 1715 Sybilla Masters was the first American woman to get a patent, for her invention of a machine for making cornmeal.

Gazette; Cornelia Bradford, who published the *American Weekly Mercury* in Philadelphia; and Mary Katherine Goddard, who first helped her mother with the *Providence Gazette* in Rhode Island and later put out the *Maryland Journal*.

Were many women writers?

Only a few women, such as Anne Bradstreet and Mary Rowlandson, published their writings, but many kept journals or wrote letters describing their activities. These journals and letters became an important source of information on early American life for later historians. Sarah Kemble Knight, for example, left a lively account of her journey on horseback from Boston to New York. In her diary Sarah Edwards recorded powerful religious experiences, describing how she felt "swallowed up in God." Still other women's journals revealed what daily life was like in the years leading up to the American Revolution.

The first known African American poet was Lucy Terry Prince, who in 1746 wrote a poem about an Indian raid in Massachusetts. The poem was not published until 1855.

REVOLUTION AND INDEPENDENCE (1760–1820)

Why were colonial women and men angry at the British? ◆ Was there a name for women who opposed the British? ◆ Why were Daughters of Liberty so strongly against drinking British tea? ◆ What was the Boston Tea Party, and did women participate? ◆ What did women do when the Revolutionary War broke out ◆ How did most women support the Revolution? ◆ Did any women fight in the war? ◆ Who were the women heroes of the Revolution? ◆ Did many womenside with the British? ◆ Did African American women support the Revolution? ◆ How did Native Americans feel about American independence? ◆ Did

Why were colonial women and men angry at the British?

In 1765 the British Parliament began taxing Americans. First the British tried to tax newspapers, then they put a tax on tea, cloth, and other supplies from England. Colonial women and men were so angry at the extra charges that they refused to buy British goods. The women brewed their own "liberty teas" from herbs and held patriotic spinning bees to make their own fabric.

Was there a name for women who opposed the British?

Just as men, calling themselves Sons of Liberty, formed secret societies to press for freedom from British laws, women organized their own protest groups, known as **Daughters of Liberty**. In addition to urging women not to buy British products, especially tea, the protesters put up posters declaring the colonists' right to liberty and signed petitions against unfair British taxes.

Why were Daughters of Liberty so strongly against drinking British tea?

Although the British stopped taxing most items, they kept the tax on tea as a symbol of their power over the colonies. Not drinking tea became a symbol of American

When one man objected to the Revolution, some Daughters of Liberty tarred and feathered him with molasses and flower petals as a punishment.

independence. At the time tea was one of the most popular drinks, so giving it up was not easy. But, as one woman wrote, "rather than Freedom, we'll part with our Tea."

When was the Boston Tea Party, and did women participate?

In 1773 Boston patriots, dressed as Indian warriors, boarded ships in the harbor and threw British tea overboard to protest ongoing British taxes. Women helped the men put on their disguises and were ready with pails of hot water to remove the war paint quickly once the deed was done.

What did women do when the Revolutionary War broke out?

As soon as the war started in 1775, women displayed their courage and commitment to the Revolution. In Pepperell, Massachusetts, for example, a group of women, led by Prudence Wright, put on men's clothes and took up pitchforks and muskets to defend their town against the advancing British. Although the British soldiers did not attack, the women captured a spy and rushed his information to the colonial forces.

How did most women support the Revolution?

Colonial women took charge of farms and businesses when their husbands, brothers, and fathers went off to war. These women kept the economy going. In Philadelphia and other cities, women went door to door raising money to support the American troops. In addition, thousands of women traveled with the troops to provide needed services. They cooked for the soldiers and helped care for the wounded. During battles they brought water and bullets to the men on the front lines.

After an attack by the British, 16-year-old Sybil Ludington mounted her horse and galloped through the Connecticut countryside at night, waking up colonists and urging them to fight.

Did any women fight in the war?

In 1776 Margaret Corbin took her husband's place when he was killed. She fired his cannon repeatedly until she was wounded. In 1778 Mary Hays put down the pitcher of water she was carrying to thirsty soldiers and ran to replace her fallen husband at his cannon. Her bravery was celebrated in the story of "Molly Pitcher," who supposedly kept firing even when a cannonball tore through her skirt.

At least one woman, Deborah Sampson, disguised herself as a man and enlisted as a soldier, under the name Robert Shurtleff. She served in the army for a year and a half and was wounded twice before anyone found out she was a woman. Some historians believe she was African American.

Who were other women heroes of the Revolution?

Several women, such as Deborah Champion, risked their lives as messengers for the Revolutionary forces. Catherine Schuyler made a dangerous trip to her family's property in Albany, New York, and destroyed the crops before the British could harvest them. In Georgia, Nancy Hart reportedly tricked five or six British supporters who tried to take her cabin. After soothing them with whiskey, she shot two and kept the others captive until neighbors came to her rescue.

In South Carolina, Emily Geiger rode 100 miles carrying a message from one American general to another. On the way she ran into a pro-British patrol, but she managed to read and swallow the message before she was searched. She delivered her report safely.

During the American Revolution, Nancy Hart shot two British loyalists who tried to seize her cabin. She kept the rest hostage until neighbors came to help. A 19th-century engraving depicts the dramatic scene.

Patriot and sculptor Patience Wright, who was in England during the war, may have hidden messages about British activities inside the wax-works she sent to America.

Did many women side with the British?

Although some colonial women were loyalists, supporting the British, they were apparently far less active than patriot women. A few formed loyalist groups, and the most adventurous became spies or messengers for the British. Ann Bates, for example, dressed as a peddler, took her wares into the American camps, and then reported on what she saw to the British.

Did African American women support the Revolution?

When the patriots shouted for freedom, many African Americans may have wondered whether it could mean freedom for them as well. But the patriots did not promise freedom for the slaves. Certainly, a number of African Americans backed the patriots anyway, but the British made an offer that was hard for slaves to refuse. The British promised freedom to any slaves who escaped and helped the loyalist cause. Thousands of men, women, and children risked their lives to take advantage of this offer.

After the Revolution the Cherokees adopted a constitution based on the U.S. Constitution. As a result, Nancy Ward lost her position on the tribal council, and there were no more "Beloved Women" (honorary women leaders).

How did Native Americans feel about American independence?

Native peoples were most concerned with their independence from the rule of white settlers. They chose whichever side they thought would grant that. One loyalist was Molly Brant, a Mohawk woman who had been the companion of the British head of Indian affairs in the North. It was she who helped convince the Iroquois to

"Give Me Liberty!"

One woman who listened carefully to the talk of freedom was a slave in a Massachusetts household, Elizabeth Freeman (or Mum Bett). In 1781 she found a lawyer, convinced him of her case, and sued for her freedom under the new Massa-chusetts constitution, which declared "all men are born free and equal." She won her own liberty plus some money for the beatings she had suffered. Her case helped lead to the outlawing of all slavery in Massachusetts in 1783.

Abigail Adams, the wife of John Adams, was a strong supporter of the Revolution. While her husband was often away on political matters, she managed the household and wrote him many thoughtful letters about American independence.

fight with the British. In contrast, Nancy Ward and her Cherokee people supported the patriots.

Did women help form the new government after the war?

In the 1700s it was not considered ladylike for women to participate in politics or even to show an interest in it. No women were invited to the 1787 convention at which the

Claiming Women's Equality

In her essay "On the Equality of the Sexes," published in Boston in 1790, Judith Sargent Murray argued that women are as smart as men. The difference, she said, was that women did not have equal educational opportunities. Murray believed that if women had more education, they could teach their children to be better citizens and would not be helpless if their husbands died (which was not unusual at the time). But Murray did not go as far as the British feminist Mary Wollstonecraft, whose 1792 book, *A Vindication of the Rights of Women,* was widely read in America. Wollstonecraft claimed that women should have the same rights as men, not only in education but also in politics.

U.S. Constitution was written. However, in a famous letter Abigail Adams (later first lady) pleaded with her husband, John Adams, to "remember the ladies" in setting up the new government. She suggested that women might start their own revolution if they had no voice in making the new laws.

Were any women allowed to vote?

Most of the new states did not let women vote, but in 1776 New Jersey gave the vote to all adults with property worth a certain amount. Married women could not vote because their husbands owned all the property, but some single women and widows qualified. A 1790 New Jersey law even referred to voters as "he or she." A good number of women voted for president in 1800, but this alarmed those in power, and in 1807 New Jersey changed its law to limit the vote to white men.

What did the early first ladies do?

The early first ladies spent much of their time managing the presidential household and entertaining visitors. As the wife of the first U.S. president, Martha Washington helped set the dignified social tone of the early presidency, although some people criticized her receptions as too regal. Her successor, Abigail Adams, was attacked for holding strong political views, but there is no clear evidence that she influenced her husband's policies.

During the War of 1812, a three-year conflict between the United States and Britain, the British set fire to Washington, D.C. Before the fire reached the White House, First Lady Dolley Madison fled, carrying a famous portrait of George Washington and important government papers.

Could girls go to school in early America?

In colonial times some girls in New England went to "dame schools," where they were taught reading, writing, and arithmetic by an older woman in her home. After the Revolution many more girls went to school. In Massachusetts, towns had to provide free elementary schools for all children after 1789. New private schools, such as the Young Ladies Academy of Philadelphia, opened to give girls a high school education. At these academies girls learned not only reading and writing, but also grammar, rhetoric, geography, history, arithmetic, and even public speaking. In addition, they might have lessons in music or dancing.

Did girls and boys go to school together?

Quakers started several boarding schools that accepted both boys and girls. There girls could study the same subjects as boys, except for Greek and Latin. But the girls and boys had entirely separate classes and did not eat or play together. Brothers and sisters could see each other, but only for a short visit every two weeks.

Could African Americans go to girls' academies?

The academies were not integrated. Some African American girls attended segregated elementary schools in the North, but secondary schools for African American girls did not open until the 1820s. Girls born into slavery in the South had almost no educational opportunities. In fact, it

From Slave to Celebrated Poet

"Snatched" (in her own words) from her parents in Gambia, Phillis Wheatley was brought to Boston as a slave at age seven. Her owners' children taught her to read, and in a few years she was writing poetry. In 1773, at age 19, she became a celebrity after a book of her poems was printed in London. She was the first African American to publish a book. Yet, even though Wheatley's writing was encouraged by her mistress, she was not freed until after her book was published. She continued to write, but died in poverty at age 31 after giving birth to her third child.

This portrait of Phillis Wheatley graced her London-printed book of poetry—the first book published by an African American.

In Baltimore in 1809 Elizabeth Seton started a new Catholic order of nuns, the Sisters of Charity of St. Joseph. Seton was considered a saint during her lifetime, and in 1975 the Catholic Church officially made her a saint, the first one born in America.

was illegal for anyone to even teach slaves to read, although a few people defied these laws.

What kind of education did Native American girls receive?

By listening to stories told by older men and women, Native American children were taught their peoples' philosophies. In addition, girls learned many skills from their mothers and other women. For example, they learned which plants had healing properties. Some girls were even trained to be shamans (spiritual healers).

Did Native American girls learn to read and write?

Missionaries, determined to convert Native Americans to Christianity, began to teach girls and boys to read and

The Shakers

The American religious community known as the Shakers was started by Ann Lee in 1776 near Albany, New York. As a young woman in England, Lee had joined the "shaking Quakers," known for their lively worship, with dancing, shouting, and shaking. Lee developed her own teachings, emphasizing a close-knit community, simplicity, charity, and equality of the sexes and races. A committed **pacifist**, she was jailed for her opposition to the Revolutionary War. After she died in 1783, Mother Lee, as she was called, was succeeded by Lucy Wright, who helped spread the Shaker teachings. The Shaker movement lasted almost two centuries, into the 1970s.

write. As early as 1727 Catholic nuns in New Orleans taught Native American girls as well as African Americans and whites.

How did women use their education?

After the Revolution many people believed that the duty of educated women was to raise good citizens (meaning male citizens). Most educated women accepted this task, but some went further and started their own schools. Others started literary clubs, and still others took up writing.

Did any women earn a living by writing?

The first woman to support herself by writing was Hannah Adams, who put together a dictionary of religions in 1784 and also wrote historical books. In the early 1790s Susanna Rowson published America's first best-selling novel. Titled *Charlotte Temple*, it described how an unsuspecting schoolgirl was seduced by a soldier, taken from her home in England to America, and then abandoned without any money. Rowson also acted on stage and later opened a girls' school in Boston.

Did many women have jobs in the late 1700s?

In the 1770s "manufacturing houses" began employing women to make cotton thread and cloth. Most women,

Mercy Otis Warren ridiculed the British in several plays published in the 1770s and later wrote a three-volume history of the American Revolution.

The first American to work at a loom run by power was probably Deborah Skinner in Waltham, Massachusetts, in 1814.

A Woman of Many Talents

One of the most knowledgeable American women in the 1700s was Susanna Wright, who died in 1784 at age 88. Born and educated in England, she helped settle the Pennsylvania frontier in 1728. She worked hard at household and agricultural chores, and in 1771 even won a prize for raising the most silkworms in Pennsylvania. Her silk was used to make a dress for the queen of England. Wright was best known, however, for her intellectual ability. She wrote poetry and corresponded with Benjamin Franklin and other important thinkers. Her neighbors often asked her to write their wills and give other legal advice. She became an unofficial judge, settling many local arguments over property. In addition, she used her knowledge of medicine to provide herbal remedies for her neighbors.

In 1800 Nancy Prosser helped her husband, Gabriel, plan a large revolt of slaves near Richmond, Virginia, but some slave owners found out and stopped the uprising.

however, continued to do household work, either in their own homes or as servants. Many women also helped with farming. In Texas and other parts of Spanish America, some women ran huge ranches. In 1790, for example, María Hinojosa de Ballí took charge of an estate that covered a third of the Rio Grande Valley.

How many women were slaves?

By 1820 more than 750,000 black women were forced to work as slaves. Most toiled on plantations, but some worked long hours in cotton mills. A few dug canals or hauled carts in the mines.

SPEAKING OUT AGAINST SLAVERY AND FOR WOMEN'S RIGHTS (1800–1870)

When did the U.S. movement for women's rights begin?

American women, led by Elizabeth Cady Stanton and Lucretia Mott, held their first large meeting to demand equal rights in 1848, in Seneca Falls, New York, but the seeds for the women's movement were planted many years earlier. From the early 1800s, women were active in a variety of women's groups through which they became involved in social issues, began voicing their opinions, and gained leadership experience.

What kinds of groups did women form in the early 1800s?

Many women joined **mutual-aid societies,** in which they paid dues into a kitty as insurance in case they got sick or lost their husbands. Other women formed charitable groups, such as the Society for the Relief of Poor Widows with Small Children in New York. Some groups emphasized education for poor children; others set up facilities for women workers. Groups called **temperance societies** tried to stop men from drinking liquor, and "moral reform" societies tried to end prostitution. Most important for the later women's movement were the women's groups that opposed slavery.

The Most Shocking Woman in America

Scottish-born Frances (Fanny) Wright defied many people's ideas of proper behavior for a woman. In 1825 she set up a model plantation in Tennessee to show how, using government land, slave owners might let slaves earn their freedom. When her experiment failed, Wright turned to other issues. In 1828 she boldly broke the long-standing social rule against women speaking to large crowds. Waving a copy of the Declaration of Independence, Wright lectured forcefully to both men and women on basic human rights. She insisted on equal opportunities for women and promoted public education for both boys and girls. Outraged by her ideas, newspapers and religious leaders called her a "female monster." Wright returned to Europe in the 1830s, but her opponents tried to belittle women's rights activists by calling them "Fanny Wrightists."

Did many African American women protest against slavery?

Every black woman in America objected to slavery, and many actively protested against it. Some women slaves resisted by running away, poisoning their masters, or setting fire to plantations or other property; many more defied slave owners by pretending to be sick, working as slowly as they could, or secretly using birth control to avoid bringing children into the world of slavery. In the North, where slavery was outlawed by the early 1800s, African American women formed anti-slavery societies and tried to help black women fleeing slavery in the South.

In 1832 Maria W. Stewart became the first American-born woman and one of the first African Americans to give public speeches against slavery and for black women's rights.

Did black and white women work together to fight slavery?

In 1832 black and white women in Boston started an anti-slavery society. The next year black and white women in Philadelphia joined forces after the American Anti-Slavery Society, a national group, refused to admit women members. Other women's anti-slavery groups formed throughout the Northeast, although some were all white and some all black.

Controversial Frances "Fanny" Wright was ridiculed for her beliefs, which included full equality for women, and for her style, which was bold and outspoken.

In 1837 about 200 women, including 20 African Americans, attended the first Anti-Slavery Convention of American Women. The next year an angry mob threatened the interracial women's convention and burned down its meeting hall at night. The women then urged all who opposed slavery to also fight racial prejudice.

Her Right to Eat with the King

Standing six feet tall and weighing 300 pounds, Kaahumanu was one of the most beautiful and most powerful women in Hawaii in the early 1800s. When her husband, the king, died in 1819, she became *kuhina nui* (coruler) with the new king. Kaahumanu stood up against many of the *kapus* (religious taboos) that restricted women's rights. At the time, for example, Hawaiian women were not allowed to eat with men, but Kaahumanu persuaded the new king to dine with her. In 1824 she announced Hawaii's first code of laws, forbidding stealing, murder, and other crimes. After learning to read and write from Protestant missionaries, Kaahumanu urged all Hawaiians to attend school, and she eventually converted to Christianity. She continued to help rule the islands until her death in 1832.

A Teacher Who Stood Up for Her Beliefs

In 1832 Prudence Crandall admitted Sarah Harris as the first African American student at a girls' school in Connecticut. White parents objected and withdrew their daughters from Crandall's classes. When Crandall then turned her school into a boarding school for African American girls, the townspeople angrily protested. Shopkeepers refused to sell food to the school, and some local residents threw stones at the school windows and even at the students. Connecticut then passed a "black law," forbidding anyone to teach African Americans from outside the state. When Crandall refused to obey this law, she was jailed. People all over the country cried out against this injustice. Crandall won her case, but the violent attacks on her school did not stop. She had to close it in September 1834.

In 1833 white Bostonian Lydia Maria Child published one of the first American books against slavery: An Appeal in Favor of That Class of Americans Called Africans. *Her book persuaded several important Bostonians, such as Senator Charles Sumner, to call for an end to slavery.*

Women were finally allowed to join the men's American Anti-Slavery Society in 1839, and they continued to protest slavery until it was abolished. Many of the women who were active in the **abolitionist**, or anti-slavery, movement later became leaders in the battle for women's rights.

Did any southern white women speak out against slavery?

From 1836 to 1838 two southern sisters, Angelina and Sarah Grimké, gave anti-slavery speeches in New England. They described the horrors they had seen as the daughters of slave owners. After Angelina wrote a pamphlet begging southern women to free their slaves, she was told never to return to the South. The Grimké sisters were attacked not just for their ideas but also for daring to voice them in public. Several ministers issued a letter warning of the dangers to a woman's character "when she assumes the place and tone of man as a public reformer." In reply, Sarah Grimké emphasized that "whatever is *right* for a man to do, is *right* for a woman to do."

Who was Sojourner Truth, and how did she get her name?

After growing up in slavery in New York, Isabella Bomefree gained her freedom in 1827, at about age 30.

FIFTH ANNIVERSARY
OF THE
MASSACHUSETTS ANTI-SLAVERY SOCIETY,
WEDNESDAY, JANUARY 25, 1837.

[☞ The public meetings, during the day, will be held in the SPACIOUS LOFT, OVER THE STABLE OF THE MARLBOROUGH HOTEL, and in the evening, in the REPRESENTATIVES' HALL.]

HOURS OF THE MEETINGS.

Meeting for Delegates at 9 o'clock in the morning, at 46, Washington-Street.

First public meeting at 10 o'clock A. M., in the LOFT OVER THE STABLE OF THE MARLBOROUGH HOTEL.

Second public meeting at 1-2 past 2 o'clock, P. M. same place.

Evening meeting at 1-2 past 6 o'clock, in the REPRESENTATIVES' HALL.

☞ The Committee of Arrangements respectfully inform the ladies that ample accommodations have been prepared for them. The loft is spacious, clean, well warmed, and will accommodate, with ease and perfect safety, at least 1000 persons.

☞ AMOS DRESSER, a citizen of this State, who was 'Lynched' at Nashville, for the crime of being an Abolitionist, will be present, and during the meetings in the afternoon and evening, will give a history of that affair.

By virtue of special compact, Shylock demanded a pound of flesh, cut nearest to the heart. Those who sell mothers separately from their children, likewise claim a legal right to human flesh; and they too cut it nearest to the *heart.—L. M. Child.*

. woman! from thy happy hearth
. . . nd thy gentle hand to save
. . e poor and perishing of earth—
. . chained and stricken slave!
. . plead for all the suffering of thy kind—
. . r the crushed body and the darkened
mind.   *J. G. Whittier.*

She was strongly religious and in 1843 had a vision telling her to become a traveling preacher. She decided to call herself Sojourner (which means traveler) and then asked God for a last name. "The Lord gave me Truth because I was to declare the truth to the people," she later said. Sojourner Truth became one of the leading African American speakers against slavery, moving many people with her call for an end to slavery. She also spoke out for women's rights.

A handbill for a meeting of the Massachusetts Anti-Slavery Society includes a quote from well-known abolitionist Lydia Maria Child.

When did women first ask the government to increase their rights?

One of the first to petition the government for women's rights was a Polish rabbi's daughter, Ernestine Rose. She came to the United States with her husband in 1836 and that year began petitioning the legislature in New York State to permit married women to own property. With Elizabeth Cady Stanton and other **feminists**, she brought petition after petition to the legislature asking for women's

In 1838 Angelina Grimké became the first woman to address a state legislature. She gave the Massachusetts legislators a petition against slavery signed by 20,000 women.

No Women Allowed

In 1840 Lucretia Mott, a Philadelphia Quaker, was one of several U.S. women delegates sent to London for the World Anti-Slavery Convention. When the women arrived, however, they were not allowed to sit with the men in the meeting hall. Instead, they had to sit behind a curtain in the balcony and could not speak to the convention. At the meeting Mott became friends with the much younger Elizabeth Cady Stanton, whose husband was a delegate. Already a budding feminist, Stanton had refused to include the traditional promise to "obey" her husband in her marriage ceremony. Mott and Stanton spent many hours walking around London and talking about the unfair treatment of the women delegates. The two women were, in Stanton's words, "resolved to hold a convention as soon as we returned home, and form a society to advocate the rights of women." Although eight years passed before they held their women's convention, the idea had been born.

economic rights. In 1848 married women won some property rights in New York State.

In 1838 the Mississippi Supreme Court agreed that, following the tradition of her Chickasaw people, Betsy Allen's property belonged to her and could not be taken to pay her white husband's debts. In 1839 Mississippi became the first state to let a married woman hold property in her own name— as long as her husband agreed.

Did any books argue for women's rights in the 1840s?

In 1845 Margaret Fuller, a leading intellectual of the time, published her book *Woman in the Nineteenth Century.* "We would have every path laid open to Woman as freely as to Man," she insisted. Soon afterward, Fuller went to Europe as a foreign correspondent for the *New York Tribune.* In Italy she joined a revolt for democracy, but had to flee when it failed. She decided to return to America with her Italian husband and child in 1850, but they all died in a storm at sea, just a few hours away from New York. She was 40 years old.

What triggered the first large meeting for women's rights?

On a visit to upstate New York in 1848, Lucretia Mott rekindled her friendship with Elizabeth Cady Stanton, who was living in that area. Stanton was unhappy with her isolated life, spent mostly taking care of her children and household matters. She, Mott, and three other women decided to put a notice in a local paper calling for a two-day "women's rights convention," July 19–20, 1848, in Seneca Falls, New York.

Who attended the first women's rights convention, and why did they come?

About 300 people, mostly women, turned out for the **Seneca Falls convention** in July 1848. Some were middle-class housewives; others worked in farms or in factories. Some were already active in the anti-slavery movement; others belonged to temperance societies, fighting alcohol abuse.

Many of these women were angry about the lack of property rights for married women, whose earnings still belonged to their husbands. As 19-year-old Charlotte Woodward put it, "Every fibre of my being rebelled [against] all the hours that I sat and sewed gloves for a miserable pittance which, after it was earned, could never be mine." Woodward wanted the right "to collect my wages."

What happened at the first women's rights convention?

In preparation for the convention Elizabeth Cady Stanton and the other organizers drafted a document that they called a "Declaration of Sentiments." Modeled on the Declaration of Independence, it began similarly, with one

Only one woman who signed the resolution at the Seneca Falls convention— Charlotte Woodward—survived to vote in 1920, the first year when all American women citizens could vote.

The Woman Who Spoke Up for the Mentally Ill

In 1843 Dorothea Dix presented a shocking report to the Massachusetts legislature. She described the horrible conditions she had seen in state prisons, where people were chained, put in cages, and whipped just because they were mentally ill.

Her account led to new hospital treatment programs for the mentally ill. For forty years, Dix continued her fight to provide better care for the mentally ill and persuaded fifteen more states to set up special hospitals for the insane.

Elizabeth Cady Stanton posed with Daniel, one of her seven children, when she was 39. Six years earlier, she had helped organize the first women's rights convention, in Seneca Falls, New York.

The chapel where the first women's rights convention was held in 1848 is still standing in Seneca Falls, New York. Nearby are the Women's Rights National Historic Park and the National Women's Hall of Fame.

important difference: It said "that all men and women are created equal" (rather than just "all men").

Voicing their determination to "throw off" any government that treated them unjustly, the women listed such injustices as having to obey laws they had no voice in making, having little chance for higher education or well-paid employment, lacking full property rights, and automatically losing custody of their children in a divorce.

When did women start asking for the right to vote?

At the Seneca Falls convention Elizabeth Cady Stanton sparked a heated debate by proposing that women be given the right to vote. Many women, including Lucretia Mott, thought that this demand was too radical, that men would use it to make fun of the women's other proposals.

Stanton, however, insisted that if women had the vote, they could put more pressure on government to accept their other demands. She was backed by the African American abolitionist Frederick Douglass, who gave a compelling speech on everyone's right to vote. By a small margin, the convention passed Stanton's resolution. It was more than 70 years, however, before women won the right to vote in all elections.

Were there many women's rights conventions in the mid-1800s?

The Seneca Falls convention sparked additional women's rights meetings in nearby Rochester, New York, as well as Ohio, Pennsylvania, Massachusetts, and other states. Two years later, in 1850, women traveled from nine states to the National Women's Rights Convention in Worcester, Massachusetts.

Who were some other early leaders of the women's movement?

Susan B. Anthony, an anti-slavery lecturer, began organizing women's rights meetings and petition drives in New York State in the 1850s. She and Elizabeth Cady Stanton became close friends and worked together to promote women's rights for more than fifty years.

The Right to Move Freely

Long skirts with layers of petticoats greatly hampered women's movements in the mid-19th century. Elizabeth Cady Stanton and her friend Amelia Bloomer were among the first women to rebel by wearing loose, puffed-out pants modestly topped by a "short" dress (which went just below the knees). When Bloomer showed this costume in *Lily*, a women's magazine she edited, the fad caught on, and the outfit was dubbed the "Bloomer costume," or just *bloomers*. But Protestant ministers and other men strongly objected to women dressing in any way like men. Stanton and other women leaders soon stopped wearing bloomers because they felt the issue of dress reform was taking attention away from more important issues, such as voting rights.

"And Ain't I a Woman?"

In 1851 Sojourner Truth gave a famous women's rights speech in Ohio. As Frances Gage, a white woman, reported, a man at the meeting ridiculed the idea of women's independence by saying that women needed "to be helped into carriages." Sojourner Truth then stood tall—about six feet tall—and exclaimed: "Nobody ever helps me into carriages, or over mud-puddles, or gives me any best place! And ain't I a woman? . . . I could work as much and eat as much as a man—when I could get it—and bear the lash as well! And ain't I a woman? I have borne thirteen children, and seen them most all sold off to slavery, and when I cried out with my mother's grief, none but Jesus heard me! And ain't I a woman?"

When Lucy Stone married Henry Blackwell in 1855, she refused to take his last name and instead kept her own. Afterward, married women who kept their maiden names were called Lucy Stoners.

Lucy Stone, another anti-slavery lecturer, also spoke out strongly for women's rights and, in Stanton's words, "stirred the nation's heart on the subject of women's wrongs." With Paulina Wright Davis, Stone organized the first National Women's Rights Convention in 1850.

Were many African American women involved in the early women's rights movement?

Only a few black women, such as Sojourner Truth and Sarah Parker Remond, attended the early women's rights conventions in the North. The most urgent cause for African American women of the 1850s was abolition of slavery, and many were actively involved in that cause. In 1850 about 1.6 million of 1.8 million black women in America were slaves. Some, such as Harriet Tubman, escaped from slavery and then helped others to escape.

How many slaves did Harriet Tubman rescue?

After escaping from slavery in 1849, Harriet Tubman bravely returned to the South almost twenty times to lead 200 to 300 slaves, including her mother and father, to freedom. She was one of the most famous conductors on the Underground Railroad, a secret, loosely organized system for guiding slaves ("passengers") to freedom in the North. Tubman constantly had to think quickly. One time,

In 1864, President Abraham Lincoln welcomed the abolitionist Sojourner Truth to the White House in appreciation for her efforts to fight slavery and help the Union army during the Civil War. She was well known as a formidable speaker with a commanding presence. If she had been shown standing next to Lincoln here, she would have been nearly his height.

when she thought slave hunters were on her trail, she did the opposite of what they expected: she took her group on a southbound, rather than a northbound, train until the danger was past. She was so effective that slave owners promised $40,000 as a reward for her capture. But she was never caught.

Did black women write against slavery in the mid-1800s?

In the 1850s Sojourner Truth and other black women published "slave narratives," telling of their experiences. Mary Ann Shadd (later Cary) put out a

Harriet Jacobs told an incredible but true story in Incidents in the Life of a Slave Girl *(1861). She detailed the abuse she endured as a slave and described how, after escaping, she hid in an attic crawl space for seven years.*

manual encouraging slaves to flee to Canada and in 1853 became the first African American woman editor, of the Canadian paper *Provincial Freeman*. Anti-slavery lecturer Frances Ellen Watkins (later Harper) spoke out for abolition in articles and moving poems, such as "The Slave Mother."

What was one of the most influential U.S. books against slavery?

Uncle Tom's Cabin, an anti-slavery novel by Harriet Beecher Stowe, a white New England woman, had a tremendous impact when it was published in 1852. It sold 300,000 copies in the first year. Stowe's depictions of the horrors of slavery fueled many northerners' determination to end this practice. In contrast, southerners denounced her book as a lie, and several southern women countered with novels defending slavery. So important was Stowe's work that when President Abraham Lincoln met her in 1862, after the start of the Civil War, he supposedly said, "So you're the little woman who wrote the book that started this big war."

When did the Civil War start, and what did women do?

The southern states withdrew their allegiance from the United States and formed their own Confederacy in February 1861. The Civil War started when Confederate soldiers captured a U.S. fort in Charleston, South Carolina,

Two Confederate Spies

At age 18 Belle Boyd began flirting with Union soldiers to gain information for the Confederates. She was imprisoned several times but kept on spying. In 1864 she was en route to England when her ship was stopped, but she promptly won the heart of her Union captor and married him in England. She later became an actress.

Using flattery, Rose Greenhow learned about the Union forces' plans and helped give the Confederates the winning edge at the first battle of Bull Run. When imprisoned, she still found ways to send information to Confederate officers. In the South she was honored as a hero and eventually paid $2,500 for her services.

The Great Escape

In late 1848 Ellen Craft and her husband, William, boldly escaped from slavery in Georgia. Ellen, who was very light-skinned, pretended to be a sick young man, "Mr. Johnson," who was traveling north with the assistance of a slave (William). She bundled up in a large overcoat and put on huge glasses, a hat, and a scarf to hide as much of her face as possible. The pair traveled to Baltimore without difficulty, but there a railroad agent refused to let "Mr. Johnson" board a train to Philadelphia without showing ownership papers for his slave. Only at the last moment did the agent relent and let the two on board. The Crafts made it safely to Philadelphia, but in 1850 they had to flee again, to England, after Congress passed a law allowing former owners to capture escaped slaves in the North.

in April 1861. On both sides, the Union in the North and the Confederacy in the South, women were vital to the war effort. They collected supplies for soldiers and served as nurses, spies, and even (in disguise) as soldiers on the battlefield. They also kept businesses and farms running while men were away fighting.

Were any women military leaders during the Civil War?

The closest to a military leader was Harriet Tubman, who served as a scout for the Union army during the Civil War. In 1863 she guided Colonel James Montgomery and several hundred African American soldiers up the Combahee River in South Carolina for a surprise attack that freed 800 slaves.

How many women fought in the Civil War?

Some historians believe that about 400 women disguised themselves as men to join the Union or Confederate army. One example was Sarah Edmonds, who, calling herself Frank Thompson, fought as a Union soldier in the battle of Fredericksburg in 1862. Because "Thompson" looked so feminine, army officers sometimes asked "him" to put on a dress and "pretend" to be a woman in order to sneak information across enemy lines. On the Confederate side

To keep people from suspecting that she ran a Union spy ring in Richmond, Virginia, Elizabeth Van Lew pretended to be slightly crazy. Her best agent was Mary Elizabeth Bowser, a freed slave who got a job in the house of Confederate leader Jefferson Davis and reported on everything she heard there.

In addition to freeing slaves through the network known as the Underground Railroad, Harriet Tubman helped the Union Army as a spy, scout, and nurse. The major African American leader Frederick Douglass was one of many people who praised her "devotion to freedom."

was Loreta Velazquez, known as Lieutenant Harry T. Buford, who fought in the first battle of Bull Run in 1861.

Were there many women nurses during the Civil War?

Hundreds of women worked as Civil War nurses, and their invaluable service helped establish nursing as a career. Dorothea Dix, known for her earlier campaign for mental hospitals, was in charge of Union army nurses. She had very strict standards and at first refused to hire attractive women under 30, but this policy did not last long.

On the Confederate side, several southern women set up hospitals in their towns, and many were active as nurses in those hospitals. Sally Tompkins, for example, ran a

Relief at the Front

Clara Barton collected and transported supplies to the battlefield. Once there she cleaned soldiers' wounds and even removed bullets. Called "the angel of the battlefield," she seemed to arrive just when her supplies and services were most needed. Mary Ann Bickerdyke also seemed a savior to many soldiers.

Known as Mother Bickerdyke, she brought in fresh food and medical supplies, did mounds of laundry, and prepared pot after pot of nourishing soup. She also assisted surgeons and took care of wounded soldiers. After two Tennessee battles in 1863, she was the only woman on hand to care for 1,700 injured soldiers.

hospital in her home in Richmond, Virginia, where she treated more than 1,300 soldiers during the war. So good was her care, only seventy-three of them died. At one point she was named a captain in the Confederate calvary just so she could continue her work.

Clara Barton spent about twenty years as a schoolteacher and patent office clerk. When the Civil War began, she organized supply deliveries for soldiers and went on to found the American Red Cross.

Were any women doctors during the Civil War?

Over some men's objections, Dr. Mary Walker was named an assistant surgeon for the Union army in Tennessee in 1863. She wore a regular officer's uniform, with a few minor adjustments, and she continued to wear trousers even after the war. Captured in 1864, she spent several months as a prisoner of war. After the war, in 1865, she became the first woman to receive the Congressional Medal of Honor.

What did women's rights activists do during the Civil War?

During the war Elizabeth Cady Stanton, Susan B. Anthony, Lucretia Mott, and many other women's rights leaders focused their energies on ending slavery. They formed the National Woman's Loyal League in May 1863 and gathered signatures in support of a constitutional amendment to end slavery throughout the United States. In fifteen months they collected an amazing 400,000 signatures. In January 1865 Congress passed the 13th Amendment, abolishing all slavery. This amendment was approved by the states by the end of 1865.

When did the Civil War end?

On April 9, 1865, Confederate general Robert E. Lee surrendered to Union general Ulysses S. Grant, bringing an end to the Civil War. Over 600,000 soldiers (probably including some women) had been killed—more Americans than in any war before or after. Women in the North and South mourned for the loved ones who had died; almost every family lost someone.

In 1867–68 Edmonia Lewis became the first African American to create a statue about the freeing of slaves. Called Forever Free, this marble sculpture now belongs to the Howard University Gallery of Art in Washington, D.C.

What did southern black women do when they were finally freed from slavery in 1865?

Because the marriages of most slaves were not legal, one of the first things freed men and women did was to find a judge or minister to perform a legal ceremony. Without a legal document, they feared someone might try to split up their families. Mothers began looking

The Hanging of Mary Surratt

After President Lincoln was fatally shot, the police moved quickly to arrest Confederate sympathizers suspected of being involved in a conspiracy with assassin John Wilkes Booth. Almost immediately they arrested Mary Surratt, a successful businesswoman who owned the boardinghouse where the plot had allegedly been hatched. The only woman among the eight accused conspirators, she repeatedly insisted on her innocence. Even though the evidence against her was very questionable, she was convicted and hanged. Two years later, it was found that the witnesses who had testified against her had lied. Today, historians agree on her innocence.

for children who had been taken away from them and sold; fathers, for sons and daughters; sisters, for brothers.

Did southern black women work after slavery ended?

Immediately after the Civil War, many African American women stopped working in the fields and put their energies into taking care of their own families and homes, but poverty soon forced a good number to return to planting and picking cotton and other crops. Now they were sharecroppers, working for a share of the crop's profit, rather than slaves, but they were still often treated brutally. Many were beaten and whipped by former owners, who were now their employers. A few single freed women, however, ran laundry businesses or even small plantations.

What was life like for southern white women after the Civil War?

Most of the Civil War was fought in the southern states, so southern women had to cope with destroyed property as well as the loss of family members. Many white women, especially from plantation-owning families, turned their anger at defeat and destruction into hatred for all northerners. For the next twenty-five years, many southern white women remained strongly opposed to women's rights activists because many of those activists came from the abolitionist movement.

What happened to the fight for women's rights after the Civil War?

In 1866 men and women abolitionists formed the American Equal Rights Association, with the goal of obtaining voting rights for both women and African Americans. The group soon divided, however, over whether to back the Republican Party's efforts to gain the vote for black men but not for women. Sojourner Truth declared that "if colored men get their rights, and not colored women theirs. . . the colored men will be masters over the women, and it will be just as bad as it was before." The debate became bitter, with Elizabeth Cady Stanton saying that an educated female voter is better than an uneducated black or immigrant male voter. Frederick Douglass,

Susan B. Anthony sits at her desk surrounded by photographs and engravings of famous women. One of the most important fighters for women's right to vote, she did not live to see all U.S. women gain this right.

Friends and Partners

When Elizabeth Cady Stanton met Susan B. Anthony in 1851, it was the start of a historic 51-year friendship and partnership that helped shape the women's movement. Stanton later commented, "We were at once fast friends, in thought and sympathy we were one, and in the division of labor we exactly complemented each other." Stanton, often busy at home with her seven children during the early years of the women's movement, wrote fiery speeches to advance women's cause; Anthony supplied Stanton with statistics and organized the campaign. "United," said Stanton, "we have a feeling of . . . such strength of self-assertion that no ordinary obstacles, difficulties, or dangers ever appear to us insurmountable."

long a supporter of women's rights, countered: "When women, because they are women, are hunted down [and killed] . . .then they will have an urgency to obtain the ballot equal to our own." Frances Ellen Harper (Watkins) and Lucy Stone agreed with Douglass, while Truth, Stanton, and Susan B. Anthony insisted that voting rights for women and African American men must be secured together.

Did African American men gain the right to vote before women?

The **15th Amendment,** passed by Congress in 1869 and approved by the states in 1870, gave black men the right to vote. It states that the right to vote may not be denied "on account of race, color, or previous condition of servitude." It would be 50 years before the 19th Amendment guaranteed that the right to vote may not be denied "on account of sex."

Were women united in their fight for the vote after the 1860s?

Not all women wanted the right to vote, and those who did split into two sides as a result of the debate over the 15th Amendment. In 1869 Susan B. Anthony and Elizabeth Cady Stanton set up the **National Woman Suffrage Association** (NWSA) to push for women's right to vote. They did not support the 15th Amendment because they

In 1868 in California a stagecoach driver known as Charley Parkhurst reportedly voted in the presidential election. About ten years later, when the stagecoach driver died, it was discovered that "Charley" was a woman: Charlotte Parkhurst.

The National Woman Suffrage Association put out a women's right weekly called the Revolution. *The American Woman Suffrage Association also had a publication, called the* Woman's Journal.

felt women should be given the vote at the same time as African American men.

Lucy Stone, writer Julia Ward Howe (best known for the lyrics of "The Battle Hymn of the Republic"), and others started a different group, the **American Woman Suffrage Association** (AWSA), which supported the 15th Amendment. Even after the 15th Amendment passed, the two groups remained separate for some twenty years.

The NWSA, considered the more radical organization, wanted to gain a constitutional amendment giving women the right to vote; it also argued for equal pay for women and better working conditions. The AWSA emphasized getting women the vote state by state rather than through a constitutional amendment. It was less concerned with working women's issues.

Where did American women have the most rights at the end of the 1860s?

During the 1868 elections women in Vineland, New Jersey, held a demonstration of their right to vote. About 175 white and black women cast ballots in a box under the eyes of a woman election "judge."

In the late 1860s women in the territory of Wyoming (which was not yet a state) had more rights than other women in America. Wyoming's new constitution, passed at the end of 1869, gave women the right to vote. The Wyoming government also gave married women the right to own property, to sign contracts, and to sue. All Wyoming men and women employed by the government or by public schools had to receive equal pay for the same work, which was very unusual at the time. In 1870 Wyoming women became the first in the country to serve on juries.

Did all girls go to school in the 1820s?

Even in the 1820s many girls from poor families did not attend school and were lucky to learn to read and write. Yet, an increasing number of girls, especially from middle-class and wealthy families, attended not only elementary schools but also secondary schools called *seminaries*. Most of these schools were private, but in 1824 the first public high school for girls opened in Worcester, Massachusetts.

What did girls' seminaries teach in the 1820s?

One of the models for many girls' schools was the Troy Female Seminary, started in 1821 by Emma Willard. There girls studied not only reading, writing, and arithmetic, but also geography, history, science, and higher mathematics. They could take classes in French, Italian, Spanish, or German, as well as in painting and dancing.

Were there any seminaries for African American girls?

Ann Marie Becroft started the first seminary for black girls in Washington, D.C., in 1820; other African American women, such as Sarah Mapps Douglass in Philadelphia, started similar schools.

Were there any Catholic girls' schools in the 1820s?

Catholic nuns were often among the first to start schools for girls, including Native American girls, on the

In the South in the 1820s it was illegal to teach slave children anything, let alone send them to school.

When teaching anatomy, Emma Willard made sure that any textbook pictures of the human body were covered over with thick paper. Young girls were not supposed to look at such shocking things.

By 1840 most American-born white women could read and write.

frontier, near the Mississippi River. In 1818, for example, Rose Philippine Duchesne opened a free school for girls in Missouri. Other nuns provided schools for poor children in East Coast cities, such as one started in 1829 in Baltimore by Elizabeth Clovis Lange (Mother Mary Elizabeth), leader of the first black Catholic community.

What did girls do after they attended the seminaries?

Although many of the girls married not long after graduating and became homemakers, a good proportion took up teaching. In Massachusetts in 1840 it was estimated that one in five of American-born white women had taught at some time.

When did women start going to college?

The first four American women went to college in 1837. That was about 200 years after the first college for men, Harvard, was started. The women studied at Oberlin College in Ohio, which promised equal education to both sexes and to all races. Three of these women—Mary Hosford, Elizabeth Prall, and Caroline Mary Rudd—gradu-

At the Hartford Female Seminary in Connecticut, opened in 1823, Catharine Beecher introduced calisthenics, a series of rhythmic exercises, to keep her students in shape.

Mount Holyoke opened as a top-notch female seminary in 1832 in western Massachusetts. Would-be students beseiged the school; soon there were more than six applicants for every first-year spot.

ated in 1841 and became the first American women with college degrees.

Were there any all-women's colleges in the 1830s?

Although there were several seminaries called "colleges," none offered an education at the level of a men's college such as Harvard. The closest to a women's college was Mount Holyoke Female Seminary in Massachusetts, opened by Mary Lyon in 1837. Young women from all economic groups were invited to apply to Mount Holyoke, but they had to pass a difficult exam to get in. They then spent three years studying grammar, algebra, geography, history, science, and other subjects. Just one year after the school opened, almost 500 women applied for 80 places.

Was it easy for southern girls to get an education in the mid-1800s?

Although the daughters of plantation owners might have governesses or attend private schools, there were few public schools open to girls in the South before the Civil War, and it was illegal to teach slaves. A few African American children got an education secretly from either a slave owner's child or a free black woman who held classes in her home.

Mary Lyon raised much of the money to start Mount Holyoke from small contributions from women.

Clara Barton's free public school, which opened in 1852 in Bordentown, New Jersey, was so successful that the town council decided it needed a male principal to run it. Barton quit.

Lucy Stone was such an excellent student that she was invited to write a speech for her graduation from Oberlin College in 1847. She refused because women were not allowed to present their own speeches; instead, her speech would have been given to a man to read.

Did the Civil War change education for girls in the South?

The number of public schools in the South greatly increased after the Civil War, adding to the opportunities for girls to get an education and for women to teach. Both the Freedmen's Bureau (a government agency) and the American Missionary Association (a Protestant group) started many schools for newly freed African Americans, both children and adults. By 1869 some 9,000 teachers, most of them women, were working in these schools. Both the teachers and the students, however, had to brave violent white mobs who opposed education for African Americans.

What was education like for pioneers in the West in the mid-1800s?

Beginning in the 1850s, many young, single Protestant women went west to teach, educating boys and girls of all ages in small one-room schoolhouses. School buildings might be literally holes in the ground, dug out of the earth, or open-air "tents" made of trees and brush. Sometimes there were desks, but often there were only uncomfortable benches. There were no standard textbooks; the children had to bring their own books, if they had any, from home. All the students were expected to learn the three R's: reading, (w)riting, and (a)rithmetic. Beyond that, the subjects studied depended on what the teacher knew and which books were available.

Did Native American girls go to school in the mid-1800s?

In the 1850s most Native American girls lived in the West, where they were educated by their own people; they did not go to formal schools or college. In the East, however, a few Native American women attended female seminaries such as Mount Holyoke and, later, colleges such as Oberlin. In 1850 the Cherokee Council and Protestant missionaries started the Cherokee Female Seminary in Indian Territory (Oklahoma). The school was supposed to reinforce Cherokee values, but it did the reverse, because most of the teachers were white Protestant women who did not approve of Cherokee traditions.

Were there many colleges women could attend in the mid-1800s?

In the 1850s women could choose a female "college" (usually a seminary) or apply to one of a few coeducational colleges, such as Oberlin or Antioch in Ohio or the University of Iowa. During the 1860s and 1870s, many new colleges opened for women. Among the new state universities to admit women were Indiana, Kansas, Minnesota, Illinois, California, Michigan, and Missouri. Other universities that accepted women included Cornell in Ithaca, New York; Howard in Washington, D.C.; and Northwestern near Chicago. New top-notch women's colleges included Vassar, upriver from New York City; Wellesley and "the Harvard Annex" (later Radcliffe), near Boston; and Smith in western Massachusetts.

Thousands of educated young women traveled west to teach in one-room schoolhouses, one of the very few careers open to women. Here Miss Blanche Lamont poses for a photograph with her students in Hecla, Montana.

Teaching Science

After gaining international attention with her discovery of a comet in 1847, Maria Mitchell taught many other women astronomers. In 1865 she set up the astronomy program at Vassar College and encouraged her students to "question everything." One of Mitchell's students was Ellen Swallow (later Richards), who in 1870 became the first woman to study at the Massachusetts Institute of Technology (MIT). (Her tuition there was free, so the president could tell the trustees she was not really a student but a guest.) In 1876 Ellen Swallow Richards set up the "Woman's Laboratory" at MIT to train women in chemistry, biology, and mineralogy. By the 1900s, however, she had shifted her energy to domestic science, or home economics.

Fanny Jackson Coppin, an early Oberlin graduate, became the highest-ranking African American woman educator in the United States in 1869, as head of the Institute for Colored Youth in Philadelphia. "Knowledge is power," she repeatedly told her students.

Who was the first African American woman to graduate from college?

Lucy Session was the first African American woman to earn a college degree, graduating from Oberlin College in 1850. Another Oberlin graduate, Sarah Jane Woodson (later Early), became the first African American woman to teach in a college, at the all-black Wilberforce University in Ohio in 1859.

Did most people approve of women going to college in the 19th century?

Although many people approved of women going to college to train as teachers, they did not think women should undertake strenuous degree programs, especially not graduate school work. *Sex in Education*, an influential book published in 1873 by Edward H. Clarke, a Harvard psychology professor, argued that if women spent too many hours studying, they would become mentally ill and lose the ability to bear children. For many years, the ideas in this book were widely accepted, especially by men.

How did people feel about women working in the 19th century?

Throughout the 1800s the image of the "lady" who stayed at home and did not go out to work was held up as the ideal for middle-class and wealthy women. Sarah Hale, editor of the *Ladies' Magazine*, and other women promoted the idea of a "woman's sphere" separate from the male world of work and politics. The reality, however, was different. Many women did work, including Hale, a widow who supported five children from her earnings, first in a hat shop and then as a writer and editor.

What kind of work did women do in the early 1800s?

Although most women did not earn money for their labor, they worked long hours in their homes in the early 1800s. Even middle-class women who had servants to help them were kept busy doing laundry, cleaning, sewing, cooking, and caring for their children. There were no automatic washers or dryers or even sewing machines before the mid-1840s. Many women lived on farms, where in addition to doing all the housekeeping, they helped with such chores as milking the cows and feeding the chickens. They also canned some of the food they raised for winter.

Although their specific duties varied from tribe to tribe, early-19th-century Native American women continued to do what they had always done: planting and harvesting crops, gathering wood or buffalo dung for fires, cooking, and caring for their children. Many women also built their own homes and made their own pots and blankets.

Popular Women's Magazines

In the early 1830s many educated women read the *Ladies' Magazine*, edited by Sarah Hale. It offered advice, poems, short biographies of famous women, descriptions of women's charity groups, and reports on advances in girls' education. Although it promised to "mark the progress of female improvement," it insisted that "meekness" was "woman's highest ornament." Another magazine, *Godey's Lady's Book,* featured pictures of the latest fashions, all carefully hand-colored by women workers. There were also poems, stories, and homemaking tips—but nothing about working women or politics. Sarah Hale became this magazine's editor in 1837; she raised subscriptions from 10,000 to 150,000 by 1860.

The 1861 cover of *Godey's Lady's Book* portrayed several ways women could help the Civil War effort: by nursing the sick, visiting prisoners, and keeping a happy home in a husband's absence.

Women of Spanish descent, who lived in parts of America that still belonged to Mexico, also spent much of their time on domestic and farm-related work. A few women worked as *llaveras* (keepers of the keys), distributing supplies and overseeing domestic activities at the Spanish missions in California and the Southwest.

Until the Civil War in the 1860s, close to 90 percent of African American women had no choice in what they did because they were held in slavery in the South.

When did white women take jobs outside the home?

The invention of the power loom in the early 1800s greatly increased the number of women working in textile mills, weaving cloth. Beginning in the 1830s in New

The Homemaker's Job

Catharine Beecher helped to define homemaking as a woman's career through her popular book *Treatise on Domestic Economy* (first published in 1841 and later revised with the help of her sister Harriet Beecher Stowe). She included detailed instructions on everything from baking a "civilized" loaf of bread to designing an efficient eight-room house. By emphasizing how women could "systematize" household work, Beecher tried to turn homemaking into a discipline worthy of study and a skilled, but womanly, profession.

England, many teenage girls (some only 11 years old) and young women went to work in these mills while their brothers and fathers stayed at home to run the farms. The women lived together in boardinghouses set up by the mill owners. Many enjoyed their independence away from home and formed close friendships. But they had to work hard, spending twelve to sixteen hours a day at their machines.

Were mill workers paid well for their work?

The young mill workers were paid only a dollar or two, perhaps three, for a week's work, and at least half of that went to pay for food and lodging in the mill company's

Through her writings, Catharine Beecher instructed hundreds of women in household work. Although she strongly supported training women to be teachers, she did not support women's right to vote.

Fighting for a Ten-Hour Day

In 1844 Sarah Bagley and other mill workers started the Female Labor Reform Association. Seeking a ten-hour workday and better working conditions, they sent a petition to the Massachusetts legislature, but their demands were dismissed.

Angered, the women successfully campaigned for the defeat of a legislator who had opposed them. The mill owners, however, forced Bagley out of her leadership role and called in police to stop further protests.

More than 40,000 teenage girls and young women worked in cotton mills by the end of the 1830s.

boardinghouses. In the mid-1830s, when the mill owners tried to cut the workers' wages, the women protested. In Lowell, Massachusetts, they formed the Factory Girls' Association in 1836. Angered by new pay cuts, about 1,500 young mill workers walked off their jobs. They marched through town and sang, "Oh! isn't it a pity, such a pretty girl as I / Should be sent to the factory to pine away and die?" Although they did not win higher wages, they inspired other women to try again later.

Did many immigrant women work in the mills?

By the late 1840s an increasing number of mill workers were immigrants, including many Irish women who came

Famed American artist Winslow Homer depicted quitting time in a 19th-century New England mill town in this drawing. Workers included children and the elderly, but most were young women.

to the United States after the potato famine of 1845–46 in their homeland. Desperate for money, these women were willing to work for very low wages, and the mill owners took advantage of this.

Did women work in other factories besides textile mills in the mid-1800s?

The invention of the sewing machine in 1846 forced many women who did sewing work at home to take factory jobs. There they toiled sixteen hours a day for a couple of dollars a week. Some women sewers in New York and Philadelphia rented space together, bought their own equipment, and shared their profits, but these cooperatives lasted only a few years.

Another invention, of a machine that stitched leather, moved many women shoemakers out of the home and into the factory in the early 1850s. The bad pay sparked a memorable, but unsuccessful, strike for higher wages in 1860. Holding signs that declared "American Ladies Will Not Be Slaves," nearly a thousand women marched with several thousand male workers through the streets of Lynn, Massachusetts, during a blizzard.

When did job opportunities for women increase?

During the Civil War (1861–65), when men went off to fight, women took their places in factories, stores, and low-

During the 1860s in Troy, New York, Kate Mullaney led several successful strikes for higher pay by women who spent twelve to fourteen hours a day washing and ironing men's detachable collars. In 1869, however, the collar workers lost a bitter strike and their union fell apart.

The Woman at the Lighthouse

In 1857, at age 15, Ida Lewis took over her father's job when he became ill and ran the lighthouse near Newport, Rhode Island. A year or two later she pulled four young men out of the water when their boat overturned. In 1869 her heroism was reported in national papers after she saved two soldiers whose boat had capsized in a storm. The public was fascinated with the story of a woman who did not even stop to put on shoes before jumping into her boat and rowing out into the rough sea to rescue the drowning men. Yet the government waited ten more years to recognize her skill. Only in 1879, after several more dramatic rescues, was she named the official lighthouse keeper.

The first national women's labor group was the Daughters of St. Crispin, organized in 1869 by women shoe stitchers in six states, from Massachusetts to California.

level government office jobs. After the war, although the surviving men took back their jobs, there was a huge growth in industry and in the total number of jobs. In the factories women continued to work mostly in the clothing industry, but some also canned foods or made cigars. For the first time women started working regularly in offices, doing typing, filing, and similar low-paid jobs. They also were hired as salesclerks, although they had to stand on their feet all day (there were no chairs or benches where they could sit down). Another new career for women was nursing; it was women who developed the standards for this profession.

What kinds of jobs were available to African American women after the Civil War?

In the South many newly freed black women continued to work in the fields, as sharecroppers rather than slaves. Other African American women worked as maids or cooks; still others worked in tobacco factories, where they were usually given the worst jobs, handling the rough tobacco leaves. An increasing number of black women, however, gained jobs as teachers, and a few began working as nurses.

Did middle-class women ever help working women in the mid-1800s?

After hearing about women sewers' difficulties, some middle-class and wealthy women formed the Working Women's Protective Union in New York City in 1868. This organization and similar groups in other cities helped women sewers both collect money they were owed and find new jobs.

Women's rights activists Susan B. Anthony and Elizabeth Cady Stanton and three other middle-class women from Working Women's Protective Unions attended the National Labor Union convention of 1868, but it was women workers, not middle-class women, who did the hard-core organizing.

When did women become doctors?

The first woman in America to receive her medical degree was Elizabeth Blackwell, in 1849. At the time most

In 1870 Augusta Lewis (later Troup) became the first woman officer of a major union, as corresponding secretary of the International Typographical Union, for male and female typesetters.

people opposed women studying medicine, so they had a difficult time getting into medical school and were often ridiculed by the male students. In 1850, for example, when Harriot Hunt was accepted by Harvard Medical School, the male students protested so much that she withdrew and the Harvard trustees later voted to refuse all women applicants (a policy that continued for almost 100 years). Hunt, a self-taught medical practitioner who had been offering Boston women medical advice since the mid-1830s, later received an honorary degree from a woman's medical college.

Did any medical schools welcome women students in the mid-1800s?

In 1850 the Female (later Woman's) Medical College of Pennsylvania opened in Philadelphia with the explicit goal of training women doctors. Yet even there police had to be called in because of angry protests at the first graduation ceremonies in 1851.

Where did the first female doctors practice medicine?

In 1853, after advanced study in Europe, Elizabeth Blackwell opened a small clinic in New York City to treat poor women, but she and other women were not allowed to work in hospitals. In 1857 Elizabeth Blackwell and two other women doctors—her sister, Emily Blackwell, and Marie Zakrzewska—started the first American hospital run by women doctors, the New York Infirmary for Women and Children. Similar hospitals run by women soon opened in Philadelphia, Boston, and Chicago.

When did women first become lawyers?

In 1869 Ada H. Kepley became the first U.S. woman to graduate from law school, in Chicago; Arabella Mansfield, in Iowa, became the first U.S. woman admitted to the bar, or practice of law.

Another early woman lawyer was Myra Bradwell, who persuaded her husband to teach her law. In 1869 she wrote a law, passed by the Illinois legislature, that gave a married woman the right to keep any money she earned, rather

Rebecca Lee (later Crumpler) became the first African American woman doctor after receiving her medical degree from the New England Female Medical College in 1864.

In 1868 in New York City Emily and Elizabeth Blackwell started a women's medical school that was the first in the United States to have a department of preventive medicine.

One of the most famous early women surgeons was Mary Harris Thompson. She founded the Chicago Hospital for Women and Children in 1865 and developed a surgical instrument that many doctors used in abdominal surgery.

The first black woman lawyer was Charlotte E. Ray. She began practice in 1872 but had a hard time finding clients who would hire her, both as a woman and as an African American.

than having to turn it over to her husband. In the same year Bradwell passed the Illinois qualifying exam for lawyers, but she was not allowed to practice. She took her case to the U.S. Supreme Court but lost. The Court's 1873 decision declared that a woman's "natural and proper timidity and delicacy" made her "unfit" for such a profession. By this time, however, the Illinois legislature had passed a new law, written by female lawyer Alta M. Hulett, opening the law and all other professions (except military ones) to women.

Were women allowed to be preachers in the 1800s?

Although the Quakers allowed women to speak at their meetings, most religions did not let women preach in the first half of the 19th century. A few women defied this ruling. Jarena Lee, for example, was not deterred when the African Methodist Episcopal (AME) Church initially refused to recognize her as a preacher. "Nothing is impossible with God," she insisted, and she succeeded in convincing AME bishop Richard Allen of her preaching abilities.

Phoebe Palmer began her preaching by holding Methodist prayer meetings for women in the mid-1830s; by 1839 men had begun to attend as well. She became one of the leaders of the Holiness movement, which believed that people could save their souls through good deeds. Her preaching and writings converted many thousands to this movement. She also called on other women to preach.

When did the first woman become a minister in a major Protestant church?

Antoinette Brown married Charles Blackwell, a brother of two of the first U.S. women doctors, Elizabeth and Emily Blackwell. Another Blackwell brother, Henry, married women's rights activist Lucy Stone.

In 1853 Antoinette Brown (later Blackwell) was ordained as the minister of a small Congregational church in northwestern New York. She soon changed her faith, however, and became a Unitarian minister. Earlier, she had studied religion at Oberlin College but was refused a degree from the divinity school because she was a woman.

Were any Catholic women religious leaders in the mid-1800s?

Although Catholic women were not (and are still not) allowed to be priests, a number of nuns established new

The First Career Women's Club

In 1868 *New York World* woman's page editor Jane Cunningham Croly, whose pen name was "Jennie June," was denied admission to a New York Press Club event because she was a woman. Her reaction was to start her own club, made up of women with careers. Called Sorosis, this club served as a kind of professional support group for its members. Croly saw clubs like hers as creating strong ties among women, and she helped to inspire many other women, with careers and without, to form clubs with different educational, social, and professional aims.

convents and schools in the 1840s and 1850s. Mother Mary Hardy, for example, started a convent in New York in 1841 and later founded Manhattanville College. On the West Coast in the mid-1850s, Sister Mary Baptist Russell set up a convent, a school, and later a hospital in San Francisco. She was not, however, the first nun in California. That honor belonged to María Dominica (born Concepción Argüello), who became known as "La Beata" ("The Blessed One") because she helped so many poor and sick people.

Were many women writers in the mid-19th century?

A surprising number of women were writers, from journalists to best-selling novelists. Susan Warner's 1851 *The Wide, Wide World*, for example, became the first American book to sell more than a million copies. Probably the most influential book of the time was Harriet Beecher Stowe's

Venezuelan-born Teresa Carreño gave her first piano concert in New York in 1862 at age 9. The next year she played one of her own compositions in Boston. She became a top pianist in the United States and Europe.

Leading Ladies

One of the best-known American actresses in the mid-1800s was Charlotte Cushman, who starred not only in traditional female parts but also in such male roles as Romeo in Shakespeare's *Romeo and Juliet*. Laura Keene, who managed her own theater company, played many leading parts while directing the other actors. (In 1865 she identified President Abraham Lincoln's assassin.) A popular comic actress was Lotta Crabtree, who became a star in the mid-1860s at age 16; she was one of the top-earning performers of her day.

Elizabeth Taylor Greenfield was a celebrated concert singer in the 1850s and was asked to sing for Queen Victoria in London; however, she was not allowed to perform operatic roles because she was African American.

In the early 1800s two sisters—Anna and Sarah Peale—were among the first women to support themselves from their paintings. Anna was known for her miniature portraits and Sarah for her full-size oil portraits.

1852 *Uncle Tom's Cabin*; it converted many readers to the anti-slavery cause. Harriet Wilson wrote *Our Nig* (1859), the first known novel by an African American woman. Among the popular fictional works for children by women were Mary Mapes Dodge's *Hans Brinker, or The Silver Skates* (1865) and Louisa May Alcott's *Little Women* (1868–69).

Were any women celebrated as singers in the mid-1800s?

Some of the most popular singers came from Europe, such as the Swedish soprano Jenny Lind, who was welcomed by a crowd of 40,000 when she arrived in New York in 1850. On the other hand, Adelina Patti, one of the top opera singers of the day, performed mostly in Europe, even though she grew up largely in New York City and made her debut there in 1859.

Who was the first well-known American woman sculptor?

In the mid-1850s Harriet Hosmer, an American living in Rome, created a sculpture titled *Puck*; it showed an elfish figure sitting on a toadstool and playing with two insects. Hosmer sold fifty copies of this piece, including one to the Prince of Wales. At one point two London art journals claimed that one of Hosmer's artworks was really created by a well-known male sculptor. Hosmer sued, and the magazines quickly took back their statements.

Statues by Women

In addition to Harriet Hosmer, several women were known for their sculptures in the 1860s and 1870s. Congress asked Vinnie Ream to do a full-size marble sculpture of President Abraham Lincoln for the Capitol in the late 1860s. In 1873 Anne Whitney also did a statue for the Capitol, of Revolutionary patriot Samuel Adams. Emma Stebbins was celebrated for *The Angel of the Waters*, which still stands as the centerpiece of the Bethesda Fountain in New York City's Central Park. Edmonia Lewis, the first known African American sculptor, male or female, shocked some critics with the realism of *The Death of Cleopatra*, which won a prize at the Philadelphia Centennial Exposition in 1876.

When did the movement west begin? ◆ Did any women join the early explorations of the Far West? ◆ Who were the first white women to go west? ◆ When did women of English descent first cross the Rockies? ◆ Did any Native American women move west in the 1830s? ◆ When did women start crossing the country in covered wagons? ◆ What was life like for pioneer women once they moved to the West? ◆ What happened to Spanish-speaking women on the frontier? ◆ Did women join the California gold rush? ◆ Were there any African Americans who went west in the mid-1800s? ◆ Were there any Chinese women in the

THE MOVEMENT WEST (1820–1900)

When did the movement west begin?

During the late 1600s and 1700s, the American frontier slowly shifted from the East Coast to the Appalachian Mountains to the Mississippi River. In 1803, overnight, the territory of the United States almost doubled in size with the Louisiana Purchase. This area, extending from the Mississippi River to the Rockies, was sold to the U.S. government by the French, who had recently acquired it from Spain. Anglo men set out to explore this new territory, and Anglo women soon joined them. The big westward push, when thousands of people crossed the Great Plains, came later, in the 1840s and 1850s.

Did any women join the early explorations of the Far West?

In 1805 Sacagawea, a Shosone woman—along with her newborn son and the French-Canadian guide who had purchased her as his wife—set out from North Dakota on the last leg of the Lewis and Clark expedition, which was exploring the newly acquired U.S. territory from the Mississippi River to the Rockies and beyond to the Pacific Coast. She acted as an interpreter with many of the native peoples they encountered, and at one point, when a canoe overturned, she saved the equipment inside it.

An Incredible Survival Story

In 1811–12 Marie Dorion, an Iowa Indian woman, traveled 3,500 miles west, from St. Louis to Oregon, with her two young boys and her husband, who was an interpreter for white explorers. In Oregon her family joined a bear-hunting expedition, and a local band of Indians attacked them. Only she and her two sons survived. She then set out for the nearest white settlement, more than 100 miles away. It was winter and a snow-storm soon forced her to stop. She and her children spent almost two cold months in a makeshift shelter of branches and snow. They had to eat their horse, but they survived.

Who were the first white women to go west?

Women of Spanish descent lived in the West for many years before those lands became part of the United States. In 1775, for example, María Feliciana Arballo y Gutiérrez journeyed 1,600 miles across the desert from her home in what is now Arizona to resettle in California.

When did women of English descent first cross the Rockies?

In 1836 Eliza Spalding and Narcissa Whitman, along with their husbands, traveled by land from Missouri to the Pacific Northwest. They were Presbyterian missionaries who wanted to convert Native Americans to their beliefs. On July 4 they became the first white women to cross the Rocky Mountains in Wyoming, although many Native American women had already done this. The entire trip took four months, with the women riding horseback most of the way.

The Spaldings settled in Idaho, where they tried to convert the Nez Percé to Christianity. The Whitmans set up a mission in Washington to teach their Presbyterian beliefs to the Cayuse. As more and more white people moved into the area, however, the Cayuse became angry; they eventually killed the Whitmans and several other missionaries.

Did any Native American women move west in the 1830s?

Native peoples were continually moving farther west as white Americans settled on their lands. Some were actually forced to move west by the U.S. government. A tragic example occurred during the winter of 1838–39, when the U.S. Army made the Cherokee people leave their homes in the Southeast and march 800 miles to so-called Indian Territory (later part of Oklahoma). Thousands of Cherokees, including many women and children, died on that long, cold trip. Quatie Ross, the wife of Chief John Ross, was one of those who did not survive. After she covered a sick child with her blanket, she became chilled and fell ill with pneumonia. Cherokees continue to remember the route to Indian Territory as *Nunna daul Tsunyi* ("the Trail of Tears" or, more precisely, "the trail where we cried").

When did women start crossing the country in covered wagons?

Beginning in 1841 wagon trains brought settlers from Independence, Missouri, to the West Coast along what was known as the Oregon Trail. The first large migration, with several hundred women, was in 1843.

What was it like for women to travel across the country in a covered wagon?

Thirteen-year-old Martha Ann Morrison (later Minto), who went west in 1844, wrote in her diary that women not only did all the cooking, but they "helped pitch the tents, helped unload, and helped yoking up the cattle." Women also collected buffalo dung as fuel for campfires. Although the men usually drove the wagons, women took over and cracked the whip if the men were sick.

Packing a Covered Wagon

It was amazing how much people were able to pack into their wagons. First, of course, were the necessities: food supplies for a journey of five to six months or more, cooking equipment, bedding, laundry supplies, clothing, rifles and ammunition, tools, barrels of water, and spare parts for the wagon. Then came the cherished pieces of furniture and other possessions. Some fully loaded wagons weighed 2,500 pounds.

A dramatic drawing portrays the dangers of prairie travel. Nevertheless, women and men flocked west, willing to make the difficult journey to better their lives.

Illness, accidents, and death were frequent occurrences on the trip west, as were births. At the beginning of her trip west in 1844, 12-year-old Catherine Sager (later Pringle) described experiencing motion sickness because of "not being accustomed to riding in a covered wagon." It took several weeks to get used to this, and the constant rain, which meant the flaps had to be kept closed, didn't make it easier. Sager's journey was especially difficult. Her mother gave birth to a girl, then became ill and died. Sager broke her leg. Her father was killed trying to turn a buffalo stampede away from the wagon. Sager and her brothers and sisters continued with the rest of the wagon train to Oregon.

What was life like for pioneer women once they arrived in the West?

Especially for the early pioneers, life on the western frontier was lonely and involved a lot of hard work. Many

A Woman Warrior

In the northern plains a Native American woman now known as Woman Chief saved a group of Crow and white families from a Blackfoot attack in the 1840s. Born to a Gros Ventre family in the early 1800s, she was captured by the Crow at age 10. Her adoptive father taught her to kill buffalo, and she took his place as the family head when he died. After halting the Blackfoot raid, she was honored as a Crow warrior and led several successful attacks on Blackfoot enemies. She was also invited to sit on the Council of Chiefs. During the 1850s she helped create peace among the tribes of the upper Missouri, but the peace lasted only a few years. In 1858 she was killed in an ambush by her original people, the Gros Ventre.

women helped build their homes and worked in the fields; they also did the cooking, laundry, and other household tasks. In northern areas, such as Montana Territory, the house might be a log cabin; on the plains of the Kansas frontier, the house was more likely to be made of blocks of sod. The nearest neighbor was often miles away.

Some women found the isolation of life on the frontier frightening and feared they might go mad, but others welcomed the challenge.

What happened to Spanish-speaking women on the frontier?

Until the late 1840s the Southwest and California were still part of Mexico. Mexican women had more property rights than American women at the time. They did not lose their property when they married and could run their own businesses as well as buy and sell crops they grew or objects they made.

All that changed, however, in 1848, when the Treaty of Guadalupe Hidalgo was signed, bringing an end to the Mexican War, between Mexico and the United States. Texas (which had been an independent republic since 1836) and the areas that are now New Mexico, Arizona, Utah, Nevada, and California, as well as half of Colorado and part of Wyoming, all became part of the United States. As a result, Mexican women became subject to the laws restricting married American women's property rights. Moreover, even women who retained their property soon lost it to the influx of white settlers.

In 1866 Clara Brown, a former slave, used money she had saved from washing miners' clothes in Colorado to start her own wagon train company to provide transportation west for African Americans who wanted to leave the South.

Did women join the California gold rush?

Some women joined the California gold rush, beginning in 1848, and earned a small fortune by setting up lodging facilities for the miners or taking in sewing or laundry.

Were there any African Americans who went west in the mid-1800s?

A number of African Americans joined the migrations in the 1840s and 1850s. After the Civil War, especially in the late 1870s and 1880s, many more fled to the West to escape white violence in the South.

One early California settler was Biddy Mason, who came to the West as the slave of a Mormon family. In 1856, when the Mormon family decided to move from Los Angeles to Texas, Mason and several other slaves won their freedom in a landmark California court case. Mason worked hard as a nurse and midwife and saved enough money to purchase her own homestead. She became wealthy through various real estate deals, helped found the First African Methodist Episcopal Church in Los Angeles, and was well known for her generosity to those in need.

Were there any Chinese women in the West in the mid-1800s?

In 1860 there were only about 1,800 Chinese women in all of the United States, but about 33,000 Chinese

A San Francisco Power Broker

An important early African American settler in San Francisco was Mary Ellen Pleasant, who arrived in 1849. She had inherited about $45,000 from her first husband, and she used this money to help the abolitionists and runaways from slavery. Eventually she started her own laundry and restaurant businesses, and one of her places was the top meeting spot for city leaders. Pleasant helped many African Americans in San Francisco to find jobs. She was also active politically, backing a law letting blacks testify in court and suing when she was told she could not ride a streetcar because she was black.

Little House in the Big Woods

Laura Ingalls Wilder turned her memories of growing up on the frontier during the 1870s and 1880s into popular stories for children. Her first book, *Little House in the Big Woods*, is loosely based on her family's life in the Wisconsin forest when she was 3 to 7 years old. Wilder also described life in Kansas (*Little House on the Prairie*), Minnesota (*On the Banks of Plum Creek*), and South Dakota (*By the Shores of Silver Lake* and other books).

men. Most of the Chinese women did not come to America by choice. The majority were kidnapped, tricked, or bought (supposedly as servants) from their families and then sold as prostitutes in America. In the mid-1870s Protestant women missionaries periodically raided the houses of prostitution to rescue the young girls and try to convert them to Christianity. In 1875 a new federal law, designed to keep Chinese women prostitutes out of the country, had the effect of keeping almost all Chinese women out.

Did many women establish their own homesteads in the West?

With the Homestead Act of 1862, the U.S. government offered 160 acres of free land to men or single women who staked out their claims and then lived on the land for five years. Although most pioneer women were married, and it was the husband who held the deed to the land, a number of widows and single young women were homesteaders. By 1910 women made up 10 percent of all homesteaders.

How did the building of the railroad affect women in the West?

Many more women traveled west after 1869, when it became possible to travel by train all the way from the Atlantic Coast, through Omaha in Nebraska, to San Francisco in California. For Native Americans and Mexican Americans already living in the West, however, the expansion of the railroad spelled an end to the life they had known. White settlers took over land that villages had held communally. Native Americans began to be herded onto reservations, and Hispanics were forced to work for the new settlers in order to survive. Mexican American women who had once worked together plastering adobe walls or baking bread for their villages now hired themselves out as servants to white settlers.

How did Native Americans feel as more and more pioneers arrived in the West?

Although at first many Native Americans helped the settlers, hostilities mounted as the number of wagons on the westward trails swelled in the 1850s. The land that the U.S. government began giving away in the 1860s was Indian land. In the late 1870s, as more and more Native Americans were forced onto reservations, several Indian women spoke up for their peoples' rights.

Who were the major Native American spokeswomen of the late 1870s?

In 1879 Susette La Flesche (later Tibbles), whose Omaha name was Inshta Theumba ("Bright Eyes"), took up the cause of Standing Bear and the Ponca people, who had been forced to leave their Nebraska lands. She joined Standing Bear on a speaking tour in the East and even spoke before the Senate to protest the Ponca removal.

Similarly, Sarah Winnemucca (later Hopkins), who had served as a scout for the U.S. Army in their 1878 war

Rosalie La Flesche Farley opposed her sister Susette La Flesche Tibbles and argued that self-government would protect the Omaha better than U.S. citizenship would. The argument ended in 1887, when Congress passed a law that essentially forced Native Americans to give up tribal ownership of their lands in return for individually owned pieces of property and U.S. citizenship.

More Women Warriors

Two Crow women (The-Other-Magpie and Finds-Them-and-Kills-Them) and a Cheyenne woman (Buffalo Calf Road) were among the warriors who fought with Sitting Bull to defend Indian lands. They bested the U.S. Army at the Battle of the Rosebud in southern Montana in 1876. Lozen and Dahteste were two Apache women warriors who fought with Geronimo to save their people's lands and later helped negotiate his surrender in 1886.

"He Changed Everything"

When she was in her mid-seventies, in 1932, Pretty-shield told a white hunter and trapper, Frank B. Linderman, about the many changes she and her Crow people had seen since the 1860s. "The happiest days of my life," she said, "were spent following the buffalo herds over our beautiful country. . . . Ahh, my heart fell down when I began to see dead buffalo scattered all over our beautiful country, killed and skinned, and left to rot by white men, many, many hundreds of buffalo." Yet she insisted, "I do not hate *anybody*, not even the white man. . . . But he changed everything for us, did many bad deeds before we got used to him."

with the Bannock people, angrily protested the treatment of her own Piute people, who were forced to march from their Nevada home to a reservation in Washington State in the winter of 1878–79. Winnemucca went to the capital to speak to the president about the injustices to her people. She also wrote a book, *Life Among the Piutes: Their Wrongs and Claims.*

Did white women speak out against the treatment of Native Americans?

In 1880 Mary Bonney and Amelia Quinton presented the president and Congress with a 300-foot-long petition

The Crime of Wounded Knee

In late December 1890 the U.S. Cavalry captured Big Foot and his people, who were on their way to the Pine Ridge Reservation in South Dakota. The Minneconjou (Sioux) group was marched to Wounded Knee Creek, South Dakota, and there they spent the night. The next morning the soldiers collected the warriors' guns. They were almost finished when a shot went off. There are different accounts about who fired the shot, but the result was that the soldiers quickly began shooting every Native American in sight. About 200 people died, including many women and children. Louise Weasel Bear later remembered, "We tried to run, but they shot us like we were a buffalo."

Women Miners

Several women joined the mining camps that sprang up from Colorado and Arizona to Alaska in the late 1800s. Most of these women set up restaurants and laundry businesses, but a few tried their hand at prospecting. Ellen E. Jack ran a prosperous silver mine in Colorado. After years of traveling to the newest mining strikes, Nellie Cashman finally got lucky in the late 1890s, with a $100,000 claim in the Yukon Territory, near Alaska.

In 1895 Mary Bong was the first Chinese woman to live in Sitka, Alaska, and possibly all of Alaska. She had many careers, including running a restaurant, working in a gold mine, and fishing for salmon alone on her eighteen-foot trawler.

with thousands of signatures, calling on the government to honor its treaties and stop white settlers from taking land in Indian Territory (now Oklahoma). Helen Hunt Jackson condemned the government's treatment of Native Americans in her book *A Century of Dishonor*, printed with blood-red covers, as well as in her novel *Ramona*.

Who was one of the wildest women of the West?

Calamity Jane, whose real name was Martha Jane Cannary, captured the public imagination with tales of her exploits in South Dakota. Beginning in 1877, her outrageous behavior was featured in dime novels about the adventures of "Deadwood Dick" and his fearless partner, "Calamity Jane." In these stories she is an expert rider and sharpshooter, ready to take on the villains of the West. In her own autobiography the real Calamity Jane presented

An Amazing Sharpshooter

Not even five feet tall and weighing less than 100 pounds, Annie Oakley (whose birth name was Phoebe Ann Moses) joined Bill Cody's Wild West Show in 1885 with her sharpshooting act. She blasted dimes that were thrown in the air and even shot cigarettes out of her husband's mouth. She was just as accurate on horseback, standing up on a galloping horse and shooting out candle flames as she raced past. Another famous trick of hers was to toss up a playing card and then riddle it with bullet holes before it could reach the ground.

Tales of Annie Oakley were hugely popular. Two women illustrators, Miss Stewart and Dorothy Hardy, made this engraving, showing Oakley's incredible shooting, for a widely read magazine.

an equally fictional account of her life. She claimed that she served as a U.S. Army scout, prospected for gold, drove stagecoaches, worked as a bartender as well as a prostitute, and married Wild Bill Hickok and at least 10 other men. What is probably true is that she often dressed as a man, occasionally worked as a "bull-cracker" whipping ox teams, drank a lot, and enjoyed shocking "good" ladies. When she died, she was buried next to Wild Bill Hickok in Deadwood, South Dakota.

Were women in the West concerned with women's rights?

Although the early leaders of the women's rights movement came from the East, it was women in the West who first gained voting rights as well as other civil rights, such as equal pay for male and female teachers. Kansas women, for example, were allowed to vote in school elections as early as 1861.

In the mid-1880s, in her fifties, Mary Fields, a former slave, worked as a freight hauler in Montana, driving a team of eight horses; in the mid-1890s she worked as a mail coach driver, delivering the mail even in blizzards. In New Mexico in the 1890s, Doña Candelaria Mestas rode a pony to deliver the U.S. mail.

Did women's rights leaders from the East go to the West to speak?

In 1867 women's rights activists Susan B. Anthony, Elizabeth Cady Stanton, and Lucy Stone all traveled to Kansas to speak about two hot issues on the state ballot: voting rights for women and for African Americans. Both measures were defeated, but two years later, at the end of 1869, the Wyoming Territory did give women the right to vote.

When did women in the West cast their first ballots?

The first Wyoming women voted in 1870, as did the first early Utah women. Kansas women gained the right to vote in at least local elections in 1887. Utah women, however, lost their voting rights in 1887 after an anti-Mormon crusade led by Methodist missionary Angelina Newman.

In 1890, when Wyoming applied for statehood, Congress asked it to restrict women's voting rights, but Wyoming legislators refused; thus, Wyoming women became the only women in the country who could vote in federal elections. In 1893 women in Colorado won the right to vote. In 1896, when Utah became a state, it restored voting rights to women. Idaho also gave women the right to vote in 1896. By 1900 women could vote in four states—Wyoming, Colorado, Utah, and Idaho—but not in any of the others.

Were any women elected to office in the West in the late 1800s?

In Kansas in 1887, the first year women could vote in local elections, Susannah Salter was elected the first U.S. woman mayor (of the town of Argonia). In Colorado in 1894, a year after women won the right to vote, three women—Clara Clessingham, Carrie Holly, and Frances Clock—were elected the first female state representatives. In Utah in 1896, Martha Hughes Cannon was elected the first woman state senator when women regained the vote there.

Why did women in the West gain the vote first? Why didn't women sue for the right to vote? ◆ How did women try to win the vote in the late 1800s? ◆ Who was the first woman to run for president? ◆ Who was the first woman to run for president? ◆ Were African American women active in the suffrage campaign of the late 1800s? What did many African American women in the late 1800s? ◆ What were working conditions like for women in the late 1800s? ◆ Did any new job opportunities open up for women in the late 1800s? ◆ Did any laws protect women workers in the late 1800s? ◆ What did middle

A Spirit of Reform (1870–1900)

Why did women in the West gain the vote first?

Historians do not agree on why the Wyoming Territory granted women the right to vote in 1869 and Utah did the same in 1870. Many scholars point out that Wyoming had relatively few eligible women voters at the time, so they did not seem a threat to the men in power there. Indeed, some scholars argue, the vote was a way of attracting women and their "civilizing" influence to the territory. In Utah, many historians suggest, the Mormons—who were the dominant religious group—wanted their women to vote in order to protect such Mormon customs as polygamy, which allowed a man to have several wives.

Why didn't women sue for the right to vote?

One woman did sue for the right to vote. In 1872 Victoria Minor filed a suit in St. Louis, Missouri, when she was not allowed to register to vote. Her case went all the way to the U.S. Supreme Court. Minor's lawyers argued that women citizens should have the right to vote under the 14th Amendment, which forbids states from enforcing laws that "abridge the privileges and immunities of the citizens of the United States." The Court, however, did not agree that the vote was a privilege of citizenship. This decision, announced in 1875, made it clear that women needed a new constitutional amendment to get the vote.

In Kansas, women were allowed to vote in school elections in 1861. Women in Michigan and Missouri gained this limited vote in 1875, followed by Massachusetts women in 1879 and New York women in 1880.

How did women try to win the vote in the late 1800s?

In the early 1870s some African American women tried unsuccessfully to vote under the new 15th Amendment, which gave African American men the right to vote. Other women refused to pay taxes, echoing the Revolutionary cry of "No taxation without representation." The main activity, however, was the formation of new state and local groups to fight for women's *suffrage*, or right to vote. In 1878 Elizabeth Cady Stanton and Susan B. Anthony arranged for a constitutional amendment on women's suffrage to be presented to Congress. This amendment was presented again and again, for forty-one years, until it was finally passed.

In 1890 a new national suffrage organization was formed, the *National American Woman Suffrage Association (NAWSA)*; it united Lucy Stone's group with Susan B. Anthony and Elizabeth Cady Stanton's group. Women got referendums on suffrage put on a number of state ballots, and in this way won the vote in Colorado in 1893 and Idaho in 1896. But there were no more victories until 1910.

Fiery activist Victoria Woodhull attracted attention and publicity with her assertive ways. An engraving shows her claiming her right to vote at the polls.

Who was the first woman to run for president?

Victoria Woodhull, an enthusiastic supporter of women's rights, decided to run for president in 1872. Earlier, she and her sister had gained attention with their successful business speculations and such startling ideas as a call for an end to all loveless marriages. In 1870 Woodhull went before the House Judiciary Committee to argue that women already had the constitutional right to vote. She also told a meeting of the National Woman Suffrage Association that women should stop at nothing to gain their rights. "We are plotting revolution," she declared. Soon, however, the leading women's rights activists shied away from Woodhull because of various scandals that surrounded her. Woodhull later moved to England.

In 1884 lawyer Belva Lockwood ran for president as the candidate of a new party organized by women, the National Equal Rights Party. "We shall never have equal rights until we take them," she claimed. She gained more than 4,000 votes and ran again in 1888.

Were African American women active in the suffrage campaign in the late 1800s?

Many African American women fought for their voting rights, but they tended to work through their own organizations rather than deal with the racism they encountered in the National American Woman Suffrage Association and other white-dominated suffrage groups.

What scared many African American women in the late 1800s?

At the end of the 19th century, many African Americans, especially in the South, lived in fear. Secret organizations for white Christian supremacy, such as the Ku Klux Klan, threatened them, especially if they were perceived as "uppity." All too often a white mob captured an African American, usually a man, but sometimes a woman, put the person's head in a noose, and hanged the person in a *lynching*.

Did any black women speak out against lynchings?

One of the most outspoken African American women of the late 1800s, and a major leader in the anti-lynching movement, was Ida B. Wells, a journalist from Memphis, Tennessee. In 1892 she wrote an angry editorial in *Free Speech*, the Memphis paper she owned, attacking the morality of white men and women after three black men

African American women were also active in fighting for civil rights, including an end to job discrimination and segregation on public transportation.

Ida B. Wells spent her life fighting against lynching and speaking out for African American rights.

were lynched. A white mob immediately destroyed the paper's offices, but luckily Wells was in the North at the time. She did not dare to return to Memphis, but she began an anti-lynching crusade from New York, going on speaking tours, setting up anti-lynching groups, and continuing to write articles exposing the crime of lynching.

In an 1887 report to a national labor union, Leonora Barry described one factory in which children as young as four worked with their mothers at sewing garments for the rich.

What were working conditions like for women in the late 1800s?

Many women, especially newly arrived Italian and Jewish immigrants, worked in garment factories or at home making artificial flowers. Polish women immigrants often took jobs in meatpacking and canning plants in the Midwest. Irish and African American women continued to

The Last Queen of Hawaii

In 1891, when Liliuokalani became queen of Hawaii, she tried to regain some of the power that had been given away to Americans. The Americans living on the islands, however, felt that her new constitution went too far, and they staged a takeover, with the help of U.S. troops, in 1893. Liliuokalani was put under house arrest and forced to give up her powers as queen in 1895.

She remained strongly opposed to making Hawaii a U.S. territory and led a movement that proclaimed "Hawaii for the Hawaiians." Congress, however, was more interested in the strategic value of these islands in the Pacific, and it voted to annex Hawaii as a territory in 1898. In her later years Liliuokalani was known as the writer of such songs as "Aloha Oe."

work as servants. African American women in the South were forced into the worst jobs in tobacco factories.

For all these women the hours were long, at least sixty to seventy hours a week and often more. The pay was low, often less than was needed for the basics of rent and food. And the conditions were appalling.

Although Hawaiian leader Liliuokalani was deposed as queen in 1895, she continued to dress and live regally. She supported Hawaii's independence from the United States.

Women in the Labor Movement

In the early 1880s some 50,000 women joined the Knights of Labor, a major national organization that actively supported women workers' rights. In the late 1880s, this group was replaced by the American Federation of Labor (AFL), which was less supportive of women workers. Nevertheless, Mary Kenney O'Sullivan became a paid organizer for the AFL. Other women started their own groups to improve women's working conditions. Collar factory worker Leonora O'Reilly, for example, organized the Working Women's Society in New York in 1886, and textile worker Elizabeth Morgan helped form the Illinois Women's Alliance in 1888.

Did any new job opportunities open up for women in the late 1800s?

Two inventions of the 1870s, the typewriter and the telephone switchboard, led to increasing employment of women typists and phone operators. By 1900 more than

Young women office workers remained something of a novelty in the late 1800s; some men regarded them as objects of amusement or derision.

three-fourths of all office workers were women. During the same period the number of women salesclerks increased more than tenfold. Few **women of color** or immigrant women, however, held either office or sales jobs.

Did any laws protect women workers in the late 1800s?

Several states passed laws limiting the hours women and children could work. Massachusetts, Illinois, and Minnesota all limited the work week for women and children to sixty hours in the mid-1870s. A major breakthrough came in 1893 when, largely in response to Florence Kelley's reports on **sweatshop** conditions, Illinois passed a law making it illegal for children under 14 to work, protecting women from working more than eight hours a day, and setting up rules to improve workplace conditions.

What did middle-class women do with their time in the late 1800s?

Middle-class women still spent much of their time on housework and child care, but inventions in the late 1800s, such as the gas stove and electric wiring, began to ease their workload. For many of these women, their main activity outside the home was membership in one of hundreds of women's clubs that formed across the country. The early clubs, in the 1870s, were primarily study clubs, focusing on literature, history, law, or other fields. In the 1880s a number of clubs shifted toward community action and social reform, such as getting kindergartens in public schools.

Clara Barton and the Red Cross

In 1881 Clara Barton set up the American Red Cross, a branch of the neutral international relief organization started by the Swiss in 1863. Almost immediately she and her coworkers were bringing food, medicine, and other supplies to victims of natural disasters throughout the United States. She was there in 1881 when a forest fire raged in Michigan and again when floods destroyed homes in the Midwest in 1884. Barton continued to direct the American Red Cross until 1904.

The Woman's Building

At the 1892–93 World's Columbian Exposition in Chicago, a special building—designed by architect Sophia Hayden—displayed women's achievements in forty-seven countries. Called the Woman's Building, it included murals by such well-known women artists as Mary Cassatt, a library with several thousand books by women, rooms of statistics about women's work, and hundreds of displays of women's creations, from embroidery and pottery to scientific inventions. The building was planned by a "board of lady managers," made up of middle-class and upper-class white women. African American women, such as activist Ida B. Wells, complained about not being asked to participate in the planning stages.

As part of the world's fair, an international meeting of women was held in 1893; it was attended by 150,000 people. Among the 330 women who spoke were longtime suffragists Lucy Stone and Susan B. Anthony, social reformer Jane Addams, and African American educators Anna J. Cooper and Fanny Jackson Coppin.

A national organization, the General Federation of Women's Clubs, united some 200 clubs in 1890.

Were 19th-century women's clubs only for white women?

Black and white women usually had separate clubs in the late 1800s. Denied membership in white clubwomen's national organizations, Mary Church Terrell in Washington, D.C., and Josephine St. Pierre Ruffin in Boston started two different national groups for African American women in the early 1890s. In 1896 these two groups merged into the National Association of Colored Women (NACW), with Terrell as the first president.

Jewish women also had their own clubs, many of which started out as charity organizations for local synagogues. In 1893 Jewish women formed the National Council of Jewish Women, which was active in social reforms.

Mexican American women joined *mutualistas* (mutual-aid societies). These organizations offered group insurance, fought against discrimination, and encouraged literacy.

Under the motto "Lifting as we climb," NACW members started day-care facilities, kindergartens, and other programs and fought for the rights of women and African Americans.

Drawings such as this helped people understand the harsh realities of child labor. Jane Addams and other women reformers crusaded against such practices.

Who was one of the leading social reformers in the late 1800s?

Jane Addams was at the forefront of the turn-of-the-century American reform movement known as the Progressive movement, which focused largely on the social problems of the cities. In 1889 in Chicago, she set up a **settlement house**—a live-in community center offering services to an immigrant neighborhood and housing for the mostly female social workers who ran those services. The idea was that by living in the house the reformers would become part of the neighborhood.

Although Addams's settlement house, called Hull House, was not the first, it became the best-known one. Addams and other residents set up classes, day-care facilities, a gym, clubs,

Hull House worker Florence Kelley helped improve conditions in sweatshops and later helped found the National Consumers' League, whose members refused to buy anything from companies that exploited their workers.

A Women's Shelter

In 1897 African American reformer Victoria Earle Matthews set up the White Rose Home in New York as a shelter for southern black women who came north looking for jobs. Often these women were offered "jobs" the minute they stepped off the train or boat; too late they learned they had been hired as prostitutes. Matthews and her staff tried to meet the women before this happened.

The First Women's Ys

White women in Boston formed the first Young Women's Christian Association (YWCA) in 1866 to provide moral support and later housing for young women who had moved to the cities to work. Four years later black women started the Philadelphia Colored Women's Christian Association. The national YWCA was organized in 1886, but white and black remained separate groups until the mid-1940s. Jewish women formed their own "Y" in the mid-1880s, in part because they felt Christian women did not understand the culture of Jewish immigrant women. Their organization was called the Young Women's Hebrew Association (YWHA).

a soup kitchen, and other services; they also promoted such reforms as factory safety, required schooling for all children, laws against child labor, better working conditions for women, juvenile courts, and cleaner streets.

Were many settlement houses started by women?

Women set up settlement houses in many different cities, as well as in some rural areas. By 1906 there were about 200 U.S. settlement houses, mostly run by women. Besides Jane Addams's Hull House in Chicago, one of the best-known centers was the Henry Street Settlement in New York, begun by Lillian Wald in 1895. Originally called Nurses Settlement, it offered a program of visiting nurses as well as many other neighborhood services.

What issue enraged many women in the late 1800s?

Thousands of women were active in the temperance movement, which aimed to stop or at least reduce the drinking of alcoholic beverages. Although temperance societies had existed since the early 1800s, the movement really took off in the 1870s. In 1873–74 a "Woman's Crusade" was mounted in Ohio, where bands of Protestant women invaded bars, praying and singing until they convinced the men inside to stop drinking. Sometimes they were successful, and bottle after bottle of liquor was poured into the gutters outside.

Soon after the Ohio crusade, Protestant women organized the **Woman's Christian Temperance Union**

Carry Nation was one of the most violent and most well known of the anti-alcohol activists. A newspaper photo shows the devout Nation kneeling and reading her Bible in one of the many jail cells she occupied after destroying bars.

(WCTU) to continue their fight. This group, which still exists today, grew to include more than 200,000 members by the end of the 1800s. Frances Willard, who became its president in 1879, energetically urged its members to fight not only against alcohol but also for such causes as moral reform and woman's suffrage.

The WCTU was a major force behind the passage of the 18th Amendment, which prohibited liquor sales, in 1919, just before women won the vote. Not all women supported the WCTU's efforts, of course, and some were later active in getting the 18th Amendment repealed (in 1933).

A Hatchet-Swinging Reformer

At the turn of the century Carry Nation took up temperance reform with a vengeance. She began by marching into bars in her Kansas hometown and singing temperance hymns until she forced all the saloons to close. Then she expanded her efforts, marching into bars throughout the state, swinging a hatchet or throwing bricks, and destroying everything within reach in what became known as a "hatchetation." She argued that she had the right to do this because Kansas had a law banning the sale of liquor, even though no one enforced it. Many people dismissed her as crazy, but she did generate a lot of publicity for the temperance cause.

A Community of Their Own

In the 1880s women in a prayer group in Belton, Texas, decided to separate themselves from "unsanctified" men, who did not share their religious beliefs. They refused to have sex with their husbands, and washed laundry, sold butter, and started other businesses to gain financial independence. After one woman was beaten by an angry husband, the group built a house for her. The women designed and built several more houses, as well as a hotel, to form an independent community called the Woman's Commonwealth.

In the late 1800s Maggie Van Cott traveled throughout the country, leading "praise meetings" and "love fests," and converting some 75,000 to her Methodist Episcopal gospel.

Were Protestant women leaders in their churches in the late 1800s?

From around 1870 to 1920 women started and directed missionary societies within the various Protestant denominations. Both black and white women served as missionaries, although they worked in separate societies. The missionary societies allowed women to assume leadership roles and also to leave home and travel abroad. Women took the Christian message to such faraway places as China and India, as well as to Native Americans and Asian immigrants in the West. The women missionaries were convinced that their beliefs were the right ones, and this conviction often prejudiced their views of other women.

Were many women preachers at the turn of the century?

Although most churches did not accept women preachers, a number of women gained reputations as evangelist preachers in the late 1800s. In her 1889 book *Woman in the Pulpit*, Frances Willard, the head of the Woman's Christian Temperance Union, counted some 500 female evangelist preachers as well as 350 Quaker women ministers.

Known as the "singing pilgrim," Amanda Berry Smith of the African Methodist Episcopal Church conducted revival meetings throughout the world. In 1878 she began a twelve-year trip to England, Liberia, and India.

Did any 19th-century women start new religious movements?

In the mid-1870s Mary Baker Eddy founded the Church of Christ, Scientist, based in Boston. Eddy's Christian Science teachings grew out of her own experience of using her faith in God to cure her physical problems, which had kept her bedridden for years. Her central belief was that only the spiritual is real—there is no material reality. In particular, she argued that sickness and pain are illusions, and thus can be overcome by prayer and faith in God. Eddy also started a major newspaper, the *Christian Science Monitor.*

Were women leaders in the Catholic and Jewish religions in the late 1800s?

Throughout the late 1800s Catholic nuns established new orders in the United States and opened schools, hospitals, and orphanages. One of the most zealous nuns was Mother Frances Xavier Cabrini, who came to New York in 1889 at the pope's request to help the many immigrants from Italy. In 1946 she was honored as the first American saint.

Although Jewish women were not allowed to be rabbis, Ray Frank (later Litman) did temporarily stand in for a rabbi in the early 1890s on the West Coast. In 1893 Jewish women held a national meeting at which they presented papers on their roles in Judaism and established the National Council of Jewish Women, to encourage social service and religious study.

Where any Native American women spiritual leaders at the turn of the century?

From the late 1800s until the mid-1930s, the U.S. government forbade Native Americans from practicing their cere-

Against Church Teachings

Eighty-year-old feminist Elizabeth Cady Stanton caused a stir in the mid-1890s by publishing *The Woman's Bible,* in which she gave her interpretation of biblical passages that were often cited to limit women's power. Church leaders condemned this work, and so did the National American Woman Suffrage Association, an organization that Stanton had helped to start. Another controversial book that attacked the church for its role in restricting women's power was *Woman, Church, and State* (1893), written by Matilda Gage, a women's rights activist who had worked closely with Stanton and Susan B. Anthony.

The Girl Who Couldn't See or Hear

As a baby, Helen Keller lost both her sight and her hearing. She also could not talk, so it was hard to let other people know what she wanted or needed. One day in 1887, when Helen was almost 7, a "miracle worker" arrived at her house: Anne Sullivan (later Macy), a teacher of blind children. Sullivan faced an incredible challenge: How do you teach someone when she or he has no sense of language, no idea that objects have names? A big breakthrough came when Sullivan pumped water over Helen's hand and spelled the letters *w-a-t-e-r* on Helen's palm. Suddenly, Helen understood that the liquid she felt on her hand had a name—*water*. Soon she wanted to know the names of everything else around her.

With Sullivan's help, Helen Keller learned to read and eventually went to Radcliffe College. She spent much of her life writing and speaking passionately on human rights issues. In 1964 she was one of the first Americans to be awarded the Presidential Medal of Freedom.

By 1890 there were about 250,000 women teachers, almost three times as many as in 1870.

monies and rituals. As a result, many Native American women experienced a loss of status, for they had often played central roles in these ceremonies. Nevertheless, some continued to be seen as holy women, as healers, and as spiritual leaders. One such woman was Blue Earring, a Lakota medicine woman in the early 1900s. As her great-grandson remembered, "When she was in a camp people were never afraid of storms. . . . Blue Earring would go out into that storm and [pray] and point her pipe, and the storm would change its path."

Did many women go to college in the late 1800s?

By 1880 almost a third of all college students were women, and this proportion continued to grow. In addition, several new women's colleges were started in the 1880s, including Bryn Mawr, near Philadelphia, and Barnard in New York.

Could women continue their education after college in the late 1800s?

In 1877 Helen Magill (later White) became the first U.S. woman to earn a Ph.D., after completing her graduate studies in Greek at Boston University. But women had few opportunities for graduate study in the 19th century. In 1885 Bryn Mawr College became the first women's college to offer graduate study, and the University of Chicago, Princeton, and Yale allowed women into their graduate programs in the 1890s. Other schools, however, were not so welcoming: Harvard University refused to give Mary Calkins a Ph.D. in psychology in 1895, even though she passed her examination and received glowing praise from William James, one of the leading American psychologists of the time.

In 1890 the Association of Collegiate Alumnae started offering financial assistance to women wishing to pursue graduate study in Europe.

What kind of educational opportunities did African American women have in the late 1800s?

The number of African Americans accepted at most colleges was very small, and some schools did not admit any. Indeed, throughout the South and in most of the rest of the country, blacks and whites were educated in separate schools. From the 1860s on, Protestant missionaries supported a number of all-black seminaries and colleges, including Atlanta Baptist Seminary (later Spelman College), which opened in Georgia in 1881 and trained many African American women as teachers and later as nurses.

What kind of schools did Native Americans attend in the late 1800s?

Many Native American children were forced to attend missionary or government schools, which punished them for speaking their native languages or practicing their people's customs. Sioux writer and activist Zitkala-Sa ("Red Bird," also known as Gertrude Bonnin) described how the "paleface" missionaries at one of these Indian schools clipped her long hair. "Our mothers," she said, "had taught us that only unskilled warriors who were captured had their hair shingled by the enemy." She tried to fight, but was tied to a chair. In her words, "I felt the cold blades of the scissors against my neck, and heard them gnaw off one of my thick braids. Then I lost my spirit."

One of the best secondary schools in the South, Haines Normal and Industrial Institute in Augusta, Georgia, was started in 1886 by an African American woman, Lucy Craft Laney, a graduate of Atlanta University.

A Great Adventure

In late 1889 reporter Nellie Bly set out to beat the record of Phineas Fogg, a fictional character in Jules Verne's popular book *Around the World in Eighty Days*. Her day-by-day account of her adventures was featured on the front page of the *New York World*. When she won her race, bettering Fogg's time by almost eight days, there was a huge celebration.

Nellie Bly (whose real name was Elizabeth Cochrane Seaman) did much more than this publicity stunt. As a young reporter, she pretended to be insane and described the horrors she saw when she was sent to a woman's insane asylum. She also went undercover to expose conditions in a sweatshop and a woman's prison.

Did Chinese American children have any problems going to school?

Most Chinese American children were kept out of white schools. For example, in 1884 in San Francisco, when Mamie Tape reached school age, she was not allowed to attend the local public school because she was of Chinese descent. Her parents took the case to court and won, but the school board got around the ruling by setting up a separate school for Chinese American children.

What opportunities were there for women in medicine at the turn of the century?

Women doctors were still not usually hired to work in existing hospitals, so they started their own hospitals, often providing much-needed services to poor areas. In the 1890s some of the top medical schools for men, such as Johns Hopkins, began to admit women students, but this led to the closing of all but three of the separate women's medical colleges by 1903. As a result, few women doctors could find teaching jobs.

The majority of women in the medical field worked as nurses, and many new nursing schools were established. In 1897 a national organization (later called the American Nurses' Association) was formed, although black nurses were effectively kept out and were forced to set up their own separate group.

In the late 1800s, Dr. Kong Tai Heong helped establish the first Chinese hospital in Honolulu, where she delivered some 6,000 babies in fifty years.

Nellie Bly was a resourceful and courageous reporter, who did not hesitate to put herself in danger to get a story. Her revelations about sweatshops and a woman's insane asylums sparked serious calls for reform.

Who was the best-known U.S. woman doctor in the late 1800s?

Mary Putnam Jacobi was the most famous American woman doctor at the end of the 19th century. In 1880 she was the first woman asked to join the prestigious New York Academy of Medicine. She published more than 100 papers during her life, including a detailed report on her own brain tumor.

After her husband became ill, Emily Warren Roebling took charge of the construction of the Brooklyn Bridge in New York, from 1872 to 1883.

Were any Native American women doctors?

Susan La Flesche (later Picotte) was the first Native American woman to receive a medical degree, from   the Woman's Medical College of Pennsylvania in 1890. She greatly improved health care on the Omaha reservation in Nebraska and started a hospital for her people. Another early Native American woman doctor was Isabelle Cole, who worked in Indian Territory (Okla-homa) in the 1890s.

Were there many inventions by women in the late 1800s?

Women patented a variety of new devices at the end of the 1800s, including several different kinds of sewing machines, a dishwasher, a safety device for elevators, and a street-cleaning cart. Probably the most important woman inventor was Margaret Knight, who in 1870 patented a machine that made square-bottomed paper bags. She also invented several shoe-cutting machines and rotary engines.

One of the most famous women composers of the turn of the century was Amy Beach, whose Gaelic Symphony *was performed in Boston, New York, and other major cities.*

Who were prominent women entertainers in the late 1800s?

The flamboyant Lillian Russell was one of the most pop-ular musical comedy stars, and in 1890 she was even asked to sing a tune, from New York, over the new long-distance phone to a listening President Harrison in Washington, D.C. A well-known opera singer was Lillian Nordica, who played grand romantic heroines in operas by Richard Wagner. As an African American, Sissieretta Jones was not allowed to perform in opera houses, but she was asked to give a spe-cial performance for President Harrison in 1892.

What sports did women play in the late 1800s?

By the late 1800s women were playing a variety of sports, from golf to basketball. Tennis was actually intro-duced to the United States by Mary Outerbridge, who learned to play it in Bermuda in 1874.

Among middle-class and wealthy women, bicycling was a popular form of exercise in the 1880s and 1890s.

The U.S. Lawn Tennis Association held its first women's singles championship in 1887. African American players were excluded from this event, so they created their own tournament, beginning in 1917.

Women began playing baseball in the early 1860s, and by the 1890s touring women's teams—called "bloomer girls" because of their outfits—took on local men's teams. One of the best-known bloomer girls was pitcher Maud Nelson, who also played third base. She went on to set up several women's teams, such as the All Star Ranger Girls. "It is worth the price of admission alone to see Miss Nelson, the phenomenal pitcher," an Oregon paper proclaimed in 1897.

"Bloomer girls," members of the Young Ladies Base Ball Club No. 1, of West Franklin, Massachusetts, pose for their 1890-91 team photo. Their striped outfits feature the bloomers that gave such teams their nickname.

Who were some great women writers in the late 1800s?

Women were some of the top children's book writers. Louisa May Alcott, for example, published almost a book a year after 1870, including *Little Men* (1871) and *Jo's Boys* (1886). Another children's classic of this time was *Little Lord Fauntleroy* (1886) by Frances Hodgson Burnett.

Sarah Orne Jewett was well known for her stories about Maine, including the novel *The Country of the Pointed Firs*

A Great Poet

When she died in 1886, Emily Dickinson left 1,775 poems, carefully bundled and dated, in the drawer of her dresser. Almost none of these poems had been published because Dickinson did not want them read while she was alive. Her sister, however, soon arranged for several volumes to be printed, and today Dickinson is considered one of the greatest American poets of all times.

Dickinson spent almost her whole life in Amherst, Massachusetts. Although she corresponded with a few other writers, she rarely saw guests after the late 1860s and did not venture out farther than her garden. Yet her life was full of emotion and wonder, as simple but powerful poems such as this one reveal:

> To make a prairie it takes
>   a clover and one bee,—
> One clover, and a bee
> And reverie.
> The reverie alone will do
> If bees are few.

In 1883 poet Emma Lazarus wrote a verse to help a fund-raising effort for the Statue of Liberty. This poem—with its famous lines "Give me your tired, your poor,/Your huddled masses yearning to breathe free"— was later inscribed at the statue's base.

(1896). More controversial was Kate Chopin's *The Awakening* (1899), which was criticized at the time for discussing women's sexuality but later became a feminist classic.

In 1891 Sophia Alice Callahan published the first known novel by a Native American woman: *Wynema: A Child of the Forest.* Two sisters, Winnifred and Edith Eaton, were the first Chinese American women to publish fiction, in 1899.

Were there any great women artists in the late 1800s?

One of the greatest American artists of the 19th century was Mary Cassatt. In the late 1870s and 1880s she showed her works in Paris with Impressionist painters such as Claude Monet and Edgar Degas. Today, almost every major American art museum has one of her paintings on display. Many of Cassatt's works portray tender, loving moments between women and children.

Among the many other important women artists at the end of the 1800s were two Native American women: Nampeyo reinterpreted ancient Hopi designs in her pottery and Datsolalee (Louisa Keyser) experimented with new designs in her baskets.

PUSHING FOR THE VOTE AND FOR PEACE (1900–1920)

Did the campaign for the vote change in the early 1900s?

Young women took on leadership roles in the women's movement and introduced new tactics. Instead of inviting women to sit quietly in large meeting halls, these women held large outdoors rallies to attract new women to the cause. In 1908 some New York women went on a "trolley car campaign," giving speaches at stops on the way to the state capital in Albany. Similarly, Illinois *suffragists* organized a "Suffrage Special" train to the state capital in Springfield, where twenty-five women give three-minute pro-suffrage speeches to the legislature.

What were some of the arguments against women getting the vote?

Many of those against women's suffrage claimed that woman's place is in the home and that only the man of the household could know enough to make decisions about the world outside the home. Some people thought that women are too illogical and would not show good judgment in voting. Another argument was that entering the world of politics would destroy women's natural "purity" and have "a dangerous, undermining effect on the character of wives and mothers," as former president Grover Cleveland put it in 1905. One underlying fear was

In 1906 Susan B. Anthony, then 86 years old, addressed the National American Woman Suffrage Association for the last time. "Failure is impossible!" she declared. Anthony had fought for more than fifty years for women's suffrage, but she did not live to vote.

The 1912 Election Day cover of popular *Leslie's* magazine portrays exuberant, stylish young suffragettes. Such favorable portrayals helped the cause of women's suffrage.

that women would no longer listen to their husbands and would take over the government. A number of people said women's suffrage would destroy the family and this in turn would destroy society.

Were any women against the vote?

Some well-to-do women were very active in the anti-suffrage movement, and many other women showed no interest in gaining the vote. The National Association Opposed to Woman Suffrage, led by Josephine (Mrs. Arthur M.) Dodge, had 200,000 members by 1915.

In 1900, led by Maud Wood Park, women college students and recent graduates started their own groups to fight for suffrage, and in 1908 they formed the National College Women's Equal Suffrage League.

Were working women involved in the suffrage movement?

In 1907 Harriot Stanton Blatch, the daughter of Elizabeth Cady Stanton, started a new suffrage group, the Equality League of Self-Supporting Women, in New York. She hoped to bring professional women such as lawyers and social workers together with factory and garment workers. Blatch served as president; the first vice president was Leonora Reilly, a labor organizer. Unlike other suffrage organizations, this group did not charge a membership fee, making it easier for working-class women to join. In the first year the group gained 19,000 members.

Were African American women active in suffrage organizations in the 1900s?

African American women, such as Ida B. Wells and Mary Church Terrell, actively campaigned for women's suffrage, but they generally worked within their own groups rather than organizations such as the National American Woman Suffrage Association. They had good reasons for this. In a speech at the 1903 NAWSA convention, white southerner Belle Kearney pointed out how woman suffrage could help counter the black male vote and in this way preserve white rule. Southern NAWSA groups were then allowed to set up their own membership criteria and did not have to admit African American women. Some white southern women later formed groups to get states to give the vote to white but not black women.

Were there any early-20th-century Mexican American feminists?

In Texas Jovita Idár, a journalist, and Soledad Peña started La Liga Femenil Mexicanista (The League of Mexican Feminists) in 1911 to fight for equal rights for all

The founding members of the National Association for the Advancement of Colored People in 1909 included such black women activists as Ida B. Wells and Mary Church Terrell and such white social reformers as Jane Addams and Mary White Ovington.

Chinese American Women's Rights Activists

Although in the early 1900s most Chinese American women were not active politically, there were exceptions. In 1902 Xue Jinqin, a Chinese student at the University of California in Berkeley, spoke to a large crowd about the need for equal rights for women and called for an end to the Chinese practice of foot binding. In 1912, soon after California women won the right to vote, Tye Leung Schulze cast her ballot in a primary election. Schulze was an interpeter for newly arrived immigrants at Angel Island, but she lost her job after marrying a white immigration officer because mixed-race marriages were not legal at the time.

At age 78 Abigail Duniway, an active suffragist for more than forty years, joined the governor in signing Oregon's official suffrage proclamation and became the first Oregon woman to register to vote.

Mexican Americans. In particular, they protested against lynchings and called for better education for Mexican American women and children.

What was the first state to give women the vote in the 20th century?

In 1910 Washington became the first state since 1896 to give women the vote. Other states soon followed. In 1911, after a heated campaign, women narrowly won the vote in California. The next year, three more states—Arizona, Kansas, and Oregon—gave women the vote.

When did women first gain the vote in the East?

In 1913 Illinois gave women partial but not full voting power by allowing them to vote for the president and municipal officials but not for statewide or congressional officers. It took four more years before women won full voting rights in an eastern state: in New York in 1917.

Dr. Anna Shaw, in cap and gown, leads a parade at a 1912 national suffrage meeting in New York City. The women carry shields with the names of states where women had gained the right to vote.

Were there any big marches for women's suffrage?

The first major suffrage parade, organized by the Equality League for Self-Supporting Women, took place in New York in 1910. Thousands of women from all economic groups marched down Fifth Avenue while even larger crowds lined the streets to watch. Although factory women had taken to the streets before in strike demonstrations, this was the first time upper-class, middle-class, and working-class women marched shoulder to shoulder in a common cause.

In March 1913 the NAWSA stole the headlines from president-elect Woodrow Wilson during inauguration week. Between 5,000 and 8,000 women, all dressed in white, marched down Pennsylvania Avenue in Washington, D.C. Some men in the watching crowd were so enraged that they attacked the women; the police did not stop them. The public and the press were horrified.

The organizers of the 1913 march in Washington, Alice Paul and Lucy Burns, both had studied in England and were inspired by the British suffragettes, who did not hesitate to provoke riots or break windows to gain headlines for their cause.

How did suffragists plan to win the vote for women in every state?

In 1916 Carrie Chapman Catt, NAWSA president, put forward what she called the "winning plan." Her goal was to get a constitutional amendment passed, so she detailed ways to put pressure on Congress. She believed that women also had to continue fighting for the vote state by state to increase the number of women who *could* vote and thus increase pressure on both Congress and the states to pass a constitutional amendment.

A different approach was taken by the other major national suffrage group, the **National Woman's Party** (NWP), headed by Alice Paul and modeled on the British suffragettes' movement. NWP women focused entirely on getting the vote at the federal level, by a constitutional amendment; they used dramatic protests to pressure the president and Congress.

Were any suffragists arrested for demanding the right to vote?

In 1917 members of the radical National Woman's Party stood outside the White House every day carrying signs with questions such as "How Long Must Women Wait for

In 1916, when President Wood- row Wilson was addressing Congress, he suddenly paused as some NWP women held up a large banner asking, "Mr. President, what will you do for woman suffrage?"

In 1919, when an African American women's club group tried to join the National American Woman Suffrage Association, it was asked to wait until suffrage passed. The white NAWSA leaders were afraid they would lose support from southern states if the black women joined.

Liberty?" After the United States entered World War I in May 1917, they used their signs to point out the contradiction in fighting to protect democracy abroad but refusing to give women full democracy at home. Some male bystanders thought the signs were unpatriotic and attacked the women; in the end, the women, not the men, were arrested. About 100 suffragists were sent to jail, where several, including Alice Paul, went on hunger strikes to protest their arrests and had to be force-fed. All of this made front-page news, and the public was shocked at the women's rough treatment. The women were then quickly released. A federal court later admitted that they had done nothing illegal and should not have been arrested.

What were the final steps in women's winning the right to vote?

In 1918 the "Anthony Amendment," giving women the right to vote, was passed in the U.S. House of Representatives, but the Senate defeated it. In the 1918 elections suffragists campaigned against four key senators who opposed the amendment, and two of them lost their seats. In 1919 both the House and the Senate approved the measure. Now it had to be approved by thirty-six states to become law. Within a week the Wisconsin, Michigan, and Illinois legislatures agreed to it, and within a year thirty-five states had approved it. Only one more was needed, but

The First Woman in Congress

In 1916—before most U.S. women could even vote—Jeannette Rankin was elected to Congress as a representative from Montana. Earlier, in 1914, she had headed the successful campaign to win the vote for Montana women. One of her first acts in Congress was to vote against U.S. entry into World War I, and she became known as a dedicated pacifist, strongly opposed to all wars. She was also known for supporting women's causes. After her first term Rankin ran for the U.S. Senate but was defeated. She continued to work in the peace movement and was reelected to Congress much later, in 1940. Again, she voted against war, casting the only vote against U.S. entry into World War II.

state after state postponed its vote. Finally, in August 1920, the measure was passed—by one vote—in Tennessee. Seventy-two years after the first women's rights convention in Seneca Falls, women won the right to vote.

Ten states did not ratify, or approve, the 19th Amendment, giving women the vote. All were southern states.

What does the amendment giving women the vote say?

The 19th Amendment states, "The right of citizens of the United States to vote shall not be denied or abridged by the United States or by any State on account of sex."

Besides the vote, what issues concerned women in the early 1900s?

Women were involved with all the major social and political concerns of the time. Thousands continued their fight for a ban on alcohol, and others continued to focus on social reforms in the cities. Many women participated in protests calling for better working conditions in factories and for laws to keep children from being forced to work. African American women protested lynching, and thousands joined a silent march down Fifth Avenue in 1917 to protest the killing of black people in race riots in Illinois. Native American, **Latina**, and Asian American women were concerned with the many restrictions on the rights of their peoples.

What difficulties did Chinese women immigrants face in the early 20th century?

The 1882 Chinese Exclusion Act prohibited most Chinese people from coming to America, and only a couple of hundred Chinese women a year entered the country before the early 1940s. Even women who were legally entitled to an entry permit had a difficult time. Beginning in 1910 they were almost automatically detained at Angel Island Immigration Station in the middle of San Francisco Bay. There they were immediately embarrassed by having to take off their clothes to be examined by a male doctor. They then were held in prisonlike facilities until they could be questioned about their backgrounds. Even if their papers were all in order, they might fail the immigration exam. As one woman with proper papers later commented, her

In the early 1900s Ida Tarbell was a leading muckraker, the name given to reporters who exposed the dirty behind-the-scenes practices of industrialists and politicians.

Picture Brides

In the early 20th century many Japanese men who were living in the United States arranged marriages by exchanging photographs with women in Japan, so their wives were called **picture brides.** In many ways this practice fit in with the Japanese tradition of marriages arranged by families. Although at the start of the 1900s U.S. laws kept out new immigrants from all Asian countries, in 1907 the Gentleman's Agreement with Japan allowed Japanese immigrants to bring family members (including new wives) to the United States. More than 20,000 Japanese women came to America as picture brides before the early 1920s, when new restrictions on immigration were enacted.

husband believed "all I needed to do was to tell the truth, [but] I told the truth and still got into trouble."

Did women take an active interest in international issues in the early 1900s?

The international issue that gained the most women supporters in the early 1900s was the call for peace, especially after World War I started. Also, there were several large meetings of European and American women on common issues concerning women's rights. In addition, women from different ethnic groups took action on issues involving their people. In the early 1900s, for example, Henrietta Szold became a leader in the Zionist movement, which called for a Jewish state in Palestine. She helped start a women's group, Hadassah, to support this cause. In 1910 a number of **Chicanas** organized support for the liberal democratic forces during the Mexican Revolution, and several Chinese American women raised money to help the 1911 Chinese Revolution, which established a brief period of democracy in China.

What did U.S. women say about peace in the early 20th century?

After World War I broke out in Europe in 1914, many American women voiced their opposition to all wars. In 1915 some 3,000 women gathered in Washington, D.C., to

Emma Goldman, a radical activist, appears here in a photograph taken during a quiet moment of study.

form the Woman's Peace Party, headed by Jane Addams. "We demand that women be given a share in deciding between peace and war," they asserted. Addams also chaired an international meeting of women in the Netherlands in 1915, where a peace committee was formed. This group later became the Women's International League for Peace and Freedom (WILPF).

Who Was Emma Goldman?

Born to a Jewish family in what was then Russia, Emma Goldman came to America in 1885, at age 16. By the early 1900s she was known as a dynamic speaker for radical causes. As an anarchist, opposed to all established forms of authority, she said she was "against everything that hinders human growth." When hecklers or police officers tried to silence her, she stood up for free speech. From 1906 to 1917 she coedited the radical magazine *Mother Earth* and wrote influential political essays. In 1917 she was jailed for opposing the wartime draft, and in 1919 she was expelled from America as a supposedly dangerous revolutionary. At the time she was called Red Emma because she supported the 1917 Russian Revolution, during which the "Reds" (Communists) overthrew the czar.

Close to 13,000 women served as "yeomanettes" in the navy and "marinettes" in the marines, mostly helping with office work.

What did American women do after the United States entered World War I?

When Congress voted to enter World War I in 1917, many American women immediately joined the war effort, although some continued to argue for peace. The Red Cross Nursing Service recruited women for the Army Nurse Corps and sent some 20,000 nurses overseas to help on the battlefront. Doctors from the American Women's Medical Association helped set up hospitals abroad, and many women did relief work overseas, assisting the multitudes of people who were left homeless and children who were orphaned.

At home women raised money and collected supplies to help the war effort. When the men went off to fight, the

Labor organizers parade through New York City on Labor Day 1910, celebrating their partial success after a major strike by women workers in of 1909–10.

women kept the iron and steel mills, arms factories, and car plants running. They also took jobs as streetcar conductors, electricians, rail yard workers, and so on.

After the war, when the soldiers returned, many women lost their wartime jobs.

Who fought for better working conditions for women in the early 1900s?

Demanding an eight-hour workday for all women and "living wages," working-class, middle-class, and upper-class women started the *Women's Trade Union League* (WTUL) in 1903. The group supported most of the strikes by women workers in the first two decades of the century, at a time when male-led national unions shied away from full support. Among the most active members were two wealthy sisters, Margaret Dreier Robins and Mary Dreier, and such labor organizers as Leonora O'Reilly, Mary Kenney O'Sullivan, Agnes Nestor, and Rose Schneiderman.

Who was Mother Jones?

Irish-born Mary Harris Jones, known as Mother Jones, became a dedicated labor organizer in the 1870s. She was especially concerned about the wrongs suffered by coal miners and by children who had to work. In the early 1900s, during a strike in Pennsylvania, she organized miners' wives to keep strikebreakers out of the mines. Armed with dishpans and brooms, these women proved a formidable force. Following Jones's advice, women who were arrested took along their babies and sang to them all night, keeping the jail keepers awake and ensuring an early release. Mother Jones made the headlines again in 1903. To protest inadequate child labor laws, she led a group of striking child workers from Pennsylvania textile mills on a 125-mile march to President Theodore Roosevelt's summer home.

Mother Jones had no fixed address; instead, she went, as she put it, wherever "there is a fight against wrong."

Were there any large strikes by women in the early 1900s?

One of the largest strikes by women took place in New York in 1909. It began as a small strike in September at two

In a large 1910 strike in Chicago, labor organizer Bessie Abramowitz (later Hillman) and other button sewers successfully rebelled against a pay cut.

shirtwaist companies, where women sewed cotton blouses that had ruffles or pleats. After they were fired for trying to unionize, the women picketed, continuing even after they were brutally beaten by police and arrested. The Women's Trade Union League supported their action, and when well-known socialite Mary Dreier was arrested, reporters wrote up the story.

In November a huge meeting was called to discuss a general strike by garment workers throughout the city. Clara Lemlich, a 16-year-old striker who had been clubbed by police, cried out, "What we are here for is to decide whether or not we shall strike. I offer a resolution that a general strike be declared—now!" The audience agreed, and soon 20,000 workers, mostly Jewish women, walked off their jobs for thirteen weeks. They won only some of their demands, but they clearly showed women's ability to walk the picket lines for an extended period.

When Maggie Lena Walker set up the St. Luke Penny Savings Bank in Richmond, Virginia, in 1903, she was both the first U.S. woman and the first African American to start a bank.

Were there any organizations for women who worked in offices?

In 1919 Lena Madesin Phillips formed the National Federation of Business and Professional Women's Clubs, which focused on improving conditions for women in the business world and increasing their employment and educational opportunities. Its original rallying cry was "At least a high school education for every business girl." The

The Business of Beauty

In the early 1900s several women were very successful in the beauty-care industry. Two made fortunes with hair-care formulas for African American women: Annie Turnbo Malone and Madame C. J. Walker. Both became self-made millionaires, and both donated money to projects that benefited the black community.

Two other women started their multi-million-dollar cosmetics empires at this time. Elizabeth Arden (whose real name was Florence Nightingale Graham) opened her first salon in New York in 1910. Her rival, Polish-born Helena Rubinstein, opened her first New York salon in 1914, after building a reputation in Europe.

Burned Alive

In March 1911 a fire broke out at the Triangle Shirtwaist Factory in New York City. The owner had locked all the doors to keep the workers at their sewing machines; the fire escapes were so rusty they fell apart; and the fire trucks' ladders could not reach the top floors. Some women were killed when they tried to jump from the windows, but most died inside. Altogether 143 women and 3 men were killed. At a memorial service labor organizer Rose Schneiderman lashed out at the public for ignoring all the women who had died over the years because of terrible workplace conditions. "Too much blood has been spilled," she declared, and she urged workers to "save themselves" by uniting in "a strong working-class movement." Some 100,000 mourners marched down Fifth Avenue after the memorial service, but the factory owners were never punished for the conditions that led to the disaster.

group gained 26,000 members in its first year and started its own magazine, *Independent Woman*.

Were there inspiring women teachers in the early 1900s?

In Kentucky, where many poor adult workers did not know how to read or write, Cora Stewart started her Moonlight School in 1911. On moonlit nights, thousands of students, from their late teens to their mid-eighties, showed up for classes.

Studying the Home

The field of "domestic science," later called home economics, was started at the turn of the century by Ellen Richards and other women. They saw the homemaker as a manager of the household and proposed ways in which she could do her job more efficiently and scientifically. They suggested, for example, how a woman could keep track of expenses and what she should do to eliminate germs. Many of the early home economics leaders had been trained in chemistry and other sciences but found it impossible to get college teaching jobs in those fields. Domestic science, which included the study of diet and nutrition, was almost the only field in which women scientists could become professors.

Most school-teachers were single women; if a woman got married while teaching, she often lost her job. It was an important victory when, in 1914, Henrietta Rodman and other New York City women won the right to continue teaching after they married.

Even though they had almost no money, several dedicated African American women teachers set up schools for black children in the South. Mary McLeod Bethune opened an elementary school for girls in 1904 in Daytona, Florida, with little more than a dollar. In the next twenty years, she added a high school and nursing and teacher training programs; she then joined forces with another school to form Bethune-Cookman College for African American women and men. In 1909 in Washington, D.C., Nannie Helen Burroughs helped start a major vocational school for black women. It encouraged students by claiming, "We specialize in the wholly impossible."

What did women do to improve health care in the early 1900s?

Many women were active as public health nurses, especially in the large cities. They visited homes, offering advice to young mothers on cleanliness and child care, and they began to set up nursing programs in schools. One woman doctor, Sara Josephine Baker, had a major impact on health in New York City. Through her public health care

Poor women with large families supported Margaret Sanger and her sister Esther Byrne (fourth and fifth from the left, respectively) before the sisters' court appearance in Brooklyn. Their birth control clinic had been shut down by the police earlier; distributing such information was illegal.

The First Birth Control Clinic

In the early 1900s it was illegal to distribute information about birth control. Margaret Sanger, however, was convinced that women needed this information. While working as a public health nurse in New York slums, she saw too many women "whose physical condition was inadequate to combat disease" become pregnant and then die. In 1914, after publishing an article arguing that contraceptives should be made legal, she fled to Europe to avoid arrest. The charges were later dropped, but Sanger was determined to offer women a choice. In 1916 Sanger, her sister Esther Byrne, and Fania Mindell defied New York laws to open the first U.S. birth control clinic. Almost 500 women came to the clinic in the ten days before the police shut it down. Margaret Sanger later founded the organization now known as Planned Parenthood.

program, begun in 1908, she cut the infant death rate in the city by more than a third.

Did any women make important medical discoveries in the early 20th century?

One woman who made a major contribution to medicine at the turn of the century was Anna Wessel Williams, who developed an important method for diagnosing rabies and a treatment for one variety of the disease diphtheria, which was common among young children at the time. Other medical detectives included Dorothy Reed Mendenhall, who discovered a way to diagnose Hodgkin's

Clubs for Girls

In 1901 Iowa schoolteacher Jessie Field Shambaugh set up two clubs, one for girls and another for boys to encourage learning about home crafts and new farming techniques. These groups were the start of today's 4-H clubs. Beginning in 1910, children could join the Camp Fire Girls, and in 1912 Juliette Gordon Low organized the first troop of Girl Scouts (originally called Girl Guides). To earn a "tenderfoot" classification, a Girl Scout had to know how to tie several knots and light a campfire, among other skills.

disease, a form of cancer; Florence Sabin, whose work added to scientists' understanding of lymph vessels; and Alice Hamilton, who became one of the world's top authorities on industrial poisons, such as lead.

Who were some top women scientists in the early 1900s?

A number of women made important contributions to astronomy as part of a Harvard College Observatory project. Williamina Fleming, Annie Jump Cannon, Antonia Maury, and Henrietta Leavitt were responsible for discovering thousands of stars and helped develop new ways of classifying them.

Other women made significant contributions to highly specialized fields, from Elizabeth Knight Britton, who wrote 350 papers on mosses, to Margaret Washburn, who published a highly regarded study of animal psychology, to Charlotte Scott, who developed new ideas in algebraic geometry.

Women scientists, however, had a difficult time at every stage of their careers. Only a few were admitted into the top graduate schools; fewer still were able to find teaching or other jobs after receiving their degrees; and even fewer were invited into the main scientific societies. The National Academy of Sciences, for example, was founded in 1863 but did not elect a woman member until 1925, when Florence Sabin was admitted.

Were any women known as explorers in the early 20th century?

Several women, usually with their husbands, traveled to uncharted areas. Harriet Chalmers Adams was probably the best known of these women. Sometimes with her husband, but sometimes on her own, she went places no white woman had ever been before. Between the 1890s and the 1930s she covered some 100,000 miles, reaching remote spots in South America, North Africa, the South Sea islands, and other parts of the world.

When did women first fly airplanes?

In 1910, seven years after the Wright brothers' historic first flight, Bessica Raiche flew a plane her husband had

In 1909, when cars were fairly new and there were no super-highways, Alice Ramsey drove cross-country with three women friends. It took them 41 days to go from New York to San Francisco, and they had to change the tires 11 times.

A Climbing Competition

Two American women set mountain-climbing records in the early 1900s. While exploring the HImalayas with her husband, Fanny Workman set a height record for women, as the first to climb a 23,300-foot mountain, in 1906. Two years later, in 1908, Annie Peck reached the top of the north peak of Mount Huascaràn in Peru and believed she had set a new record. Workman, however, sent a scrientific team to determine the mountain's height, and they found it was only 21,800 feet, well under Workman's record. Although Peck lost the contest, the peak was named Cumbre Ana Peck in her honor. A committed suffragist, Peck stuck a banner reading "Votes for women" at the top of 21,250-foot Peruvian peak in 1911. She was 61 years old at the time.

built. In 1911 Harriet Quimby became the first U.S. woman to get a pilot's license, and in 1912 she was the first woman to fly across the English Channel. But she died not long afterward, when she was thrown from her open cockpit in midair (there were no seat belts).

A few women of color were among the early aviators. Anna Low, the first Chinese American woman to fly, took to the air in 1919, although she did not have a license. Bessie Coleman became the first U.S. woman to earn an international pilot's license, in 1921, after being denied a U.S. license because she was an African American. A popular stunt pilot, Coleman died in 1926 when she, like Harriet Quimby, was jolted out of her plane.

Crowds loved to watch stunt pilot Blanche Scott as she flew upside down or dove 4,000 feet and then suddenly leveled out.

Did any women direct films in the early 1900s?

In 1910 French-born Alice Guy Blaché started a U.S. film company and directed several hundred short films. Lois Weber, who started directing films in 1913, often made strong political statements, as in *Shoes* (1916), which was against child labor. Another early woman filmmaker, Nell Shipman, trained animals to star in her wildlife adventures.

What did women write about in the early 1900s?

Women wrote all kinds of fiction, from historical romances to murder mysteries to autobiographical stories to experimental works. They also wrote biographies of

The Barefoot Dancer

Isadora Duncan broke all the rules with her new style of dance in the early 1900s. Kicking off traditional ballet shoes and wearing loose, revealing robes, she tried to show her audiences how beautiful a woman's moving body can be. At the time that was shocking to most American audiences, but Europeans admired her daring dances. Duncan was known for wearing a long, flowing scarf, but one scarf killed her. It got caught in the spokes of a car wheel and broke her neck when the car started moving.

Film star Mary Pickford, called America's Sweetheart, often played a poor little orphan in a cold, mean world. In real life, she was a clever businesswoman, who cofounded a major film company, United Artists.

famous women, comic and tragic plays, and powerful poems. One of the major fiction writers of the period was Willa Cather, who portrayed strong female characters in her novels about life on the Nebraska frontier, *O Pioneers!* (1913) and *My Antonia* (1918). Another important fiction writer, Edith Wharton, described the social conflicts in upper-class New York society at the turn of the century. Today she is probably best known for such classics as *Ethan Frome* (1911) and *The Age of Innocence* (1920).

Were there any women architects in the early 1900s?

Julia Morgan was one of the best-known architects in California, where she designed some 800 buildings. She established her reputation when she rebuilt the Fairmont Hotel in San Francisco after the 1906 earthquake. Today she is probably best known for designing San Simeon, William Randolph Hearst's castle along the California coast.

FROM FLAPPERS TO DEPRESSION AND WAR (1920–50)

What were flappers? ◆ Were flappers the only women rebels in the 1920s? ◆ What did women do after they won the vote? ◆ Were women elected to government positions in the 1920s? ◆ What laws helped women in the 1920s? ◆ Did most women in the 1920s want a law that said men and women were the same in all rights? ◆ How did African American women use the vote in the 1920s? ◆ Were American women active in international politics in the 1920s? ◆ Did women writers express the spirit of the 1920s? ◆ Who was the most important woman artist in the 1920s? ◆ Were any women national heroes in the 1920s? ◆ What was

What were flappers?

Flappers were young, mostly middle-class women in the 1920s who rebelled against earlier images of women. They abandoned the long skirts, layers of petticoats, and tight corsets that had greatly restricted women's movement during the 1800s and early 1900s. Instead, they wore short, above-the-knee skirts or even knickers (knee-length pants). Many cut off their long hair in favor of a short, easy-to-care-for "bob." Their behavior was equally defiant: They smoked in public, just like men; they drove their own cars; and they kicked up their heels to dance, not the staid waltz, but the lively Charleston. Flappers were not content to sit quietly at home; they wanted to be out in the world having a good time.

Were flappers the only women rebels in the 1920s?

Although flappers captured public attention, other women rebelled against traditional roles in the 1920s. In politics women were elected or appointed to new state and federal positions, and they formed new organizations to make their voices heard. Women workers continued to fight for better conditions, while other women, such as scientist Florence Sabin, proved their abilities in "men's" areas.

In the eyes of the public the perfect flapper was Clara Bow, star of the 1927 film It. With her impish good looks and fun-loving attitude, she definitely had "it"—sex appeal.

What did women do after they won the vote?

After winning the vote in 1920, the leaders of the suffrage movement continued to be active politically. The National American Woman Suffrage Association started a new organization, the League of Women Voters. This organization joined other large women's groups to lobby the government for improved health care for infants, laws protecting women workers, better public schools, and other reforms. The radical National Woman's Party, led by Alice Paul, pushed for an *Equal Rights Amendment*, giving women full equality—especially equal pay.

In the 1920s women held at most 2 percent of the elected government positions.

Were women elected to government positions in the 1920s?

Ten women won seats in the House of Representatives in the 1920s, although most were wives or daughters of previous representatives. In 1924 two women were elected governor: Nellie Tayloe Ross in Wyoming and Miriam ("Ma") Ferguson in Texas. Both succeeded their husbands in office. Florence Allen was the first woman elected to a state supreme court, in Ohio in 1922.

Also in 1922, Rebecca Felton of Georgia, then in her early eighties, made headlines when she was appointed to serve for one day as a U.S. senator, finishing the term of a senator who had died. The first woman elected to the Senate was Hattie Caraway of Arkansas, who was appointed to her late husband's seat in 1931 and then won in her own right in 1932. She served in the Senate until 1945.

What laws helped women in the 1920s?

Women won two major legislative victories in the 1920s. The first was the Sheppard-Townsend Act, passed in 1921 as a result of women's lobbying efforts. Under this law, the federal government funded public health clinics that provided care for mothers and their infants, before and after birth. Some 3,000 clinics were set up and run mostly by women, but the program's funding was cut off in 1929.

Until 1931 American-born Asian women lost their citizenship if they married Asian men.

The second victory was the Cable Act in 1922. Before this law was passed, if an American-born woman married a foreigner, she automatically lost her U.S. citizenship. Now a U.S. woman who married a foreigner could keep her citizenship—unless she married a foreigner who was not eligible for citizenship, such as an Asian.

It was not until 1923 that women were able to practice law in all forty-eight states.

Did most women in the 1920s want a law that said men and women had the same rights?

Women disagreed on the proposal for an Equal Rights Amendment, which stated that "men and women shall have equal rights throughout the United States." Supporters believed that this amendment would end all discrimination against women. Opponents, including most women union leaders, argued that it would hurt women workers by eliminating laws that protected them from long hours and that it would, in practice, make women less equal. The amendment never came up for a vote in the 1920s, but it was revived later, in the 1940s and again in the 1970s.

How did African American women use the vote in the 1920s?

Actually, most African American women were not allowed to vote at all. Although the 19th Amendment supposedly gave all women citizens the right to vote, black women in southern states were often denied their rights. When they went to register, they had to pass a literacy test, prove that they had paid property taxes, or overcome some other obstacle. African American women complained to the League of Women Voters and the National Woman's Party, but neither group was willing to challenge these restrictions.

What problems concerned African American women in the 1920s?

African American women faced discrimination in work, education, and housing, as well as voting. They also feared for their lives. Race riots occurred in several cities, resulting in murders and the destruction of black homes and businesses. Lynchings continued, and African American women, such as Mary Talbert, who headed the NAACP's Anti-Lynching Crusaders, campaigned against this brutality. By 1930 they succeeded in persuading some southern white women to take a strong stand against

On average in the 1920s, a white woman earned 61 cents, but a black woman only 20 cents, for every dollar a white man earned.

lynching in a new organization called the Association of Southern Women for the Prevention of Lynching.

Were American women active in international politics in the 1920s?

A number of women were involved in the peace movement and the call for arms reduction. In 1921, for example, they pressured President Warren Harding to sponsor an international disarmament meeting, and in 1928 they successfully lobbied Congress to sign an international agreement that condemned the use of war. Many of the peace activists came under attack as Bolsheviks (supporters of the Russians), but they disregarded this red-baiting.

Did women writers express the spirit of the 1920s?

Poet Edna St. Vincent Millay conveyed the enthusiasm for a full and active life of many young women in the 1920s. In her most famous poem, she wrote, "My candle burns at both ends, / It will not last the night; / But, ah, my foes, and oh, my friends / It gives a lovely light!" She became the first woman to win the Pulitzer Prize in poetry, in 1923.

Several African American women writers, such as Georgia Douglass Johnson, Jessie Fauset, and Zora Neale Hurston, were leaders in the Harlem Renaissance, an outpouring of black creativity in the 1920s and early 1930s. In

The Highest Honor for Peace

In honor of years of work as head of the Women's International League for Peace and Freedom, Jane Addams was awarded the Nobel Peace Prize in 1931. She was the first U.S. woman to receive this honor. In one of her many writings on the need for worldwide peace, Addams said, "I should like to see the women of civilization rebel against the senseless wholesale human sacrifice of warfare. I am convinced that many thousands of women throughout the world would gladly rise to this challenge." Addams was also well known for campaigning for social reforms and democratic freedom, and she helped found the American Civil Liberties Union in 1920.

Two Native American Activists

In different ways, Zitkala-Ša (Gertrude Bonnin) and Alice Jemison spoke out for their peoples' rights. A well-regarded Sioux writer, Zitkala-Ša served on the board of the Society of American Indians until it folded in 1920. She then persuaded the General Federation of Women's Clubs to sponsor her research into the government's treatment of Native Americans. She also spoke to many women's clubs about the need for Indian citizenship. In addition, in 1926 she founded the National Council of American Indians and lobbied government officials for reforms.

Alice Jemison was both a journalist and one of the most active Native American lobbyists of the 1930s. During this time she was the main spokesperson of the Seneca people and later the American Indian Federation in Washington, D.C. She strongly opposed the Bureau of Indian Affairs and any government involvement in tribal affairs.

poems, novels, plays, paintings, and sculptures, black writers and artists, women and men, defined a truly African American culture, just as the music of the Jazz Age did.

Who was the most important woman artist in the 1920s?

Georgia O'Keeffe, one of the greatest American artists of the 20th century, painted some of her most famous works in the 1920s. O'Keeffe had first shown her work in New York in 1916, at an experimental art gallery run by photographer Alfred Stieglitz, whom she later married. During the 1920s she did huge close-ups of flowers such as the painting *Red Poppy* (1927). Later, she turned to southwestern scenes, such as large, white animal bones in a desert.

Of her work Georgia O'Keeffe said, "When I was still a little girl, I used to think that since I couldn't do what I wanted to . . . at least I could paint as I wanted to and say what I wanted to when I painted."

Did any women become major religious leaders in the 1920s?

The most prominent woman preacher in the first half of the 20th century was an evangelist, Aimee Semple

In New Mexico, starting in the 1920s, María Martínez won many prizes at the Santa Fe Indian Market for her black pottery. Her work influenced many other Native American artists.

The Blueswomen

The music that defined the 1920s was jazz, especially the songs known as blues. African American women were some of the top blues singers, with numbers such as "Crazy Blues" by Mamie Smith and "Down-Hearted Blues" by Bessie Smith, who was called the Empress of the Blues. In their songs these women expressed their feelings about almost every aspect of their lives. There were blues about floods and sickness and death, about loneliness and love gone wrong, but there were also blues about happy times and having fun. There were "Money Blues" and "Bedbug Blues" and "Toothache Blues," but there were also defiant blues, with titles like "Don't Mess with Me" and "I Ain't Gonna Play No Second Fiddle."

McPherson, who founded the International Church of the Foursquare Gospel in Los Angeles in 1923. Every night close to 5,000 people gathered to hear her speak. Her performances were dramatic—announced by a huge band and choir. McPherson set up a variety of services to help those in need, from an employment bureau to telephone counseling. A mystery arose in 1926 when she suddenly disappeared and then turned up in Mexico, claiming she had been kidnapped. The government believed this was a hoax and filed fraud charges against her, but these were later dropped. By 1944, when she died, McPherson's church had 400 American and Canadian branches and more than 22,000 members.

Were any women national heroes in the 1920s?

In 1928 Amelia Earhart was celebrated as a hero and given a ticker-tape parade when she became the first woman to fly across the Atlantic. On this flight she served as a standby pilot on a crew with two men. But Earhart was a talented pilot in her own right, and in 1932 she proved her skill by becoming the first woman to fly alone across the Atlantic. Three years later, she made the first solo flight by any pilot from Hawaii to the U.S. mainland. In 1937 Earhart set off from Miami, with Frederick Noonan as her navigator, for a flight around the world. They reached New

In 1926 Gertrude Ederle was the first woman to swim across the English Channel; she beat the best male swimmer's time by two hours.

Amelia Earhart set many flying records and was one of the ninety-nine women pilots who started the ninety-nines Club in 1929. Congress honored her with the Distinguished Flying Cross in 1932.

Guinea and then took off on the most dangerous part of their trip, aiming for a tiny island in the Pacific. Earhart and Noonan never reached this island; they disappeared and, to this day, no one knows what happened.

What was the Great Depression, and how did it affect women?

The Great Depression was a severe economic crisis that began in 1929 and lasted throughout the 1930s. All over the country women and men lost their jobs as factories, stores, and other businesses shut down. Women of color were the hardest hit.

Did the government do anything to help people during the Great Depression?

The government set up a huge public works program to provide jobs, but male workers were usually the first to

Many African American women in cities organized housewives' leagues and used their buying power to support black businesses and firms that hired black workers. Their efforts grew into a national "Buy Where You Can Work" campaign to force businesses to hire African Americans.

This photograph by Dorothea Lange, taken in 1938, shows a young California farm worker at a rally for strikers, who were trying to raise their wages from 75 cents to 90 cents for picking 100 pounds of cotton.

be hired. In addition, Congress passed a law establishing minimum wages and maximum hours, and many women workers got pay raises as a result. This law, however, excluded **domestics** and agricultural workers—meaning most women of color.

Did women workers call for better conditions during the 1930s?

Throughout the 1930s working women of all ethnicities—Chinese, Japanese, African, Mexican, Polish, Russian, Jewish, Italian—joined unions, increasing their membership threefold. In some cases, even during the depression years, women staged successful strikes. In 1933 in St. Louis, for

Images of the Depression Years

Many of the photographs that shaped people's image of the depression years were taken by women. Dorothea Lange's photograph of a migrant worker with her children came to symbolize human suffering during the depression. Margaret Bourke-White published equally powerful photographs in her book with Erskine Caldwell, *Have You Seen Their Faces?* A very different photograph by Bourke-White, of a huge dam in Montana built under a federal relief program, was on the cover of the very first issue of *Life* magazine, in 1936.

A Radical Catholic

In 1933 Dorothy Day and Peter Maurin started the Catholic Worker movement, which emphasized taking direct action on issues of social justice. Day edited the movement's paper, *The Catholic Worker*, which sold for a penny and published important leftist writers. To provide shelter and food for the poor, Day and Maurin opened "houses of hospitality." Day continued her fight for social justice for almost fifty years.

example, black women pecan workers walked out, demanding the same pay and conditions that white women workers had. They were joined by the white workers, who refused an offer of more pay from the employers, and they won.

Women also supported men's strikes. In 1937, when Michigan autoworkers held a sit-down strike inside the factory, the Women's Emergency Brigade brought the men food, picketed, and fended off the police. This strike gave birth to the United Auto Workers (UAW) union.

During the Great Depression the government forced thousands of people of Mexican descent, including many U.S. citizens, to leave the United States for Mexico.

Were there any women labor leaders in the 1930s?

Most of the major unions were led by men, but a few women held important positions. In the garment industry, Rosa Pesotta and Dorothy Bellanca were vice presidents on the boards of the two major unions, but they were

Surviving in the Depression

Without women's efforts, many families would not have survived during the depression. Wherever they could, women cut back on household and food costs, following the lead of First Lady Eleanor Roosevelt, who insisted on seven-cent meals at the White House. To add to the family income, they took on odd jobs, such as washing clothes, selling home-baked bread, or styling hair. One woman, whose husband was often out of work, said, "I did what I had to do. I seemed to always find a way to make things work. I think hard times is harder on a man, 'cause a woman will do something. Women just seem to know where they can save or where they can help, more than a man."

At a 1939 meeting in Alabama, Eleanor Roosevelt refused to sit in the "white" section and moved her chair so that it was in both the white and "black" sections.

exceptions. Luisa Moreno began organizing Latina pecan shellers in the late 1930s, as well as other agricultural and cannery workers; during the 1940s she was a vice president of a major union, but was later deported.

Who was the most important American woman during the 1930s?

Many people agree that the most influential U.S. woman during the 1930s and later was Eleanor Roosevelt, the first lady from 1933 to 1945. Because her husband, President Franklin Delano Roosevelt, was crippled by polio, she often toured the country as his representative and reported on the problems she saw, influencing his policies. She quickly became known as a champion of the poor and oppressed, and she spoke out strongly for the civil rights of African Americans.

Eleanor Roosevelt was a tireless traveler on behalf of her husband Franklin, who was confined to a wheelchair by polio. Her support for women's and African American rights earned her admirers and more than a few critics.

Eleanor Roosevelt also did much to promote women. Beginning in 1933, she held her own press conferences and invited only women reporters. As a result, many newspapers had to hire female journalists. Together with Mary Dewson, a top Democratic Party campaigner, Eleanor Roosevelt successfully urged the appointment of women to important government jobs. She also encouraged women to discuss political issues through her own newspaper column, "My Day."

During World War II Eleanor Roosevelt argued for women's participation in the war effort and equal treatment of African American soldiers. After her husband's death and the end of the war, she continued to serve her country. She was the only female U.S. delegate to the new United Nations and was one of the main voices in creating the Universal Declaration of Human Rights. When this declaration was passed by the UN General Assembly in 1948, she was given a standing ovation.

In 1934 Florence Allen was appointed as the first woman federal judge, on the court of appeals. In her autobiography she noted that one male judge was so upset he supposedly stayed in bed for two days.

Who were some of the top women in President Franklin Roosevelt's government?

Frances Perkins, named secretary of labor in 1933, was the first woman in the cabinet, made up of the president's top advisers. During her twelve years in this job she helped write many major laws benefiting workers, including the Social Security Act.

One of several women who ran government aid programs during the Great Depression was Ellen Woodward, in charge of emergency relief for the more than 500,000 women who headed their households. Ruth Owen in 1933 became the first U.S. woman envoy (much like an ambassador) to a foreign country (Denmark).

The Chinese Women's Patriotic Association protested the 1932 invasion of China by Japan as well as discrimination in the United States against Chinese Americans.

Did African American women hold government positions in the 1930s?

The top-ranking African American woman in government was Mary McLeod Bethune, the director of the Division of Negro Affairs in the National Youth Administration. A leading educator and organizer within the black community, she brought together a group of mostly male African American government officials, known

Crystal Bird Fauset became the first African American woman elected to a state legislature, in Pennsylvania in 1938.

Mary McLeod Bethune, center, was a major African American leader and helped organize an unofficial "black cabinet" to advise the president.

as the black cabinet, to promote policies benefiting African Americans. She also organized a strong coalition of black women's groups, called the National Council of Negro Women, to fight for both civil rights and women's rights.

Were Mexican American women active in politics in the 1930s?

In 1929 María Hernández and her husband, Pedro, started a group in Texas to push for Mexican American civil rights. Other women were active in such reform groups as the League of United Latin American Citizens. Concha Ortiz y Pino de Kleven was the first Chicana elected to a state legislature, in New Mexico in 1936.

What did women write about in the 1930s?

Jane Bolin was appointed the first African American woman judge, in New York City in 1939.

Women wrote about almost everything. Pearl Buck described the life of a hardworking peasant family in China in *The Good Earth* (1931). She won the Pulitzer Prize for this book and in 1938 became the first American woman to be awarded the Nobel Prize in literature. Margaret Mitchell published *Gone with the Wind* (1936), a historical romance set in the South of the Civil War period and after. It was an immediate hit, selling 50,000 copies in one day, and was soon made into a popular movie. From a very different perspective, Zora Neale Hurston portrayed the problems facing a young African American woman in the South in her novel *Their Eyes Were Watching God* (1937).

Many women wrote children's books, including such classics as *Little House in the Big Woods* by Laura Ingalls Wilder and the many Nancy Drew mysteries by "Carolyn Keene" (a pseudonym for several writers, but mostly Harriet Stratemeyer Adams).

Who starred in the movies in the 1930s?

Many of the best-known classic film stars appeared in the 1930s, including Greta Garbo, Marlene Dietrich, Bette Davis, and Joan Crawford. Child star Shirley Temple (later Black) was named the "outstanding personality of 1934" at the Academy Awards. Katharine Hepburn made the spunky Jo of Louisa May Alcott's *Little Women* come to life on the screen; she also starred in several other films portraying independent women.

Did women have the same rights as men by the 1940s?

Although by the early 1940s women had made many gains, they did not have full legal equality with men. In some states, a married woman was still not allowed to sign a contract, and in a few places a husband could take

In the early movies African American women were given only such stereotyped parts as maids. Hattie McDaniel made the best of this situation to become the first African American to win an Oscar, for her role as Mammy in Gone with the Wind *(1939).*

A Symbolic Concert

In 1939 singer Marian Anderson was supposed to give a concert in Washington, D.C., at Constitution Hall. But the group that owned the building, the Daughters of the American Revolution (DAR), refused to let her sing there because she was an African American. First Lady Eleanor Roosevelt was outraged and helped arrange for a concert at the Lincoln Memorial. There, on Easter Sunday, Anderson performed for 75,000 people, and many more listened on the radio. This event became a symbol for the civil rights struggle. Later, in 1955, Anderson became the first African American to sing at the Metropolitan Opera.

his wife's earnings. Women were not allowed to serve on juries in about half the states, and in some states they could not run for governmental office. In addition, the average man still earned much more than the average woman. For all these reasons, a number of women's groups urged Congress to pass the Equal Rights Amendment in the mid-1940s. Labor activists, however, strongly opposed the measure, believing it would undo hard-won protections for women workers, and it was defeated.

How did World War II affect women?

One of the most important affects of World War II was to greatly increase the number of working women, at least during the wartime period. Between 1942 and 1945 about 6 million new women workers started jobs. In addition to doing such traditional women's work as sewing, they built airplanes and ships, mined copper, staffed steel and lumber mills, and worked on the railroads.

To urge women to join the war effort, posters and magazines displayed pictures of a fictional young woman called Rosie the Riveter, dressed in overalls with her sleeves rolled up, ready for work. Women were told that cutting out a dress pattern was similar to cutting out airplane parts and running an electric mixer was like operating a drill.

What happened to women's jobs after the war?

When the war ended in 1945 and male soldiers returned home, many women lost their jobs. In Detroit, for example, women made up a fourth of the autoworkers

About 2,000 women joined the Women's Air Service Pilots, which helped the army by flying new planes from the factories to the bases, training male pilots, and testing planes that were having mechanical difficulties.

Wartime Work for Women Ballplayers

During World War II, while top men players were away fighting, women were hired to entertain sports fans. The All-American Girls Baseball League, begun in 1943, actually lasted well after the war, until 1954. About 600 women played on ten teams. They came from all over the country, and a few were even from Cuba; African American players, however, were not allowed. To make the team, the women had to not only prove their athletic skills but also attend a charm school, where they learned how to put on makeup and pose for the media.

during the war, but afterward their numbers dropped to less than a twelfth. Women were now encouraged to support their country by staying at home and raising a family.

Did women join the army and navy in World War II?

About 350,000 women served in the armed forces during the war, and many more provided supporting services. Some 140,000 joined the **Women's Army Corps (WAC)**; most did office work, but a few served in intelligence and other nontraditional areas. Another 100,000 women signed up with the navy's **WAVES** (short for Women Accepted for Volunteer Emergency Service or, as some women phrased it, Women Are Very Essential Sometimes). Many thousands of women also joined the Army Nurse Corps and Navy Nurse Corps. A number of women, mostly nurses, died while serving their country; others were captured and held as prisoners of war.

Could any woman join the military during World War II?

Although African American women could join the Women's Army Corps, they were segregated from white enlistees. For most of the war, black women were kept out of the WAVES. The number of black nurses allowed into

During World War II hundreds of thousands of women volunteers helped the U.S. forces at home and abroad. These women did everything from raising money by selling war bonds to driving ambulances.

Japanese Americans during the War

After the Japanese attacked Pearl Harbor in December 1941, many Americans expressed anger toward anyone of Japanese descent. Beginning in 1942 the U.S. government forced more than 110,000 Japanese Americans, living on the West Coast, into prisonlike camps. Families had to abandon their homes, quickly sell their belongings, give away their pets, and resettle in uncomfortable housing behind barbed-wire fences.

Mitsuye Edo, claiming she was being held in the camps against her will, petitioned the government for her freedom. Her case went to the Supreme Court, which ruled that her detention was illegal in late 1944, the day after the government ended its internment policy.

Margaret Fukouka, a private in the Women's Army Corps, was one of the many Japanese Americans who served their country during World War II, even though the U.S. government put some Japanese American families in camps behind barbed-wire fences.

the Army Nurse Corps was severely limited, and the Navy Nurse Corps did not admit them at all.

Other women of color also faced discrimination, but Native American, Latina, and Asian American women all served during the war.

Did any women report on World War II?

During World War II, for the first time, a number of women journalists filed reports from the front. Ann Stringer even managed a scoop, as the first to report the historic joining of Russian and U.S. forces in 1945. Margaret Bourke-White took her camera on a bombing mission and with American troops first venturing into Germany. She also helped publicize the horrors of the concentration camps with her photographs taken when the inmates were first released.

What did African American women do to end discrimination in the late 1940s?

Two black women won important Supreme Court decisions for civil rights in the late 1940s. In 1947 Irene Morgan refused to sit in the section designated for African

In 1934 foreign correspondent Dorothy Thompson was considered such a threat that she was thrown out of Germany for her anti-Nazi columns.

Americans at the back of a bus going from Virginia to Maryland. After hearing her case, the Supreme Court declared segregation on interstate transportation illegal.

In 1948 Ada Lois Sipuel (later Fisher), an Oklahoma resident, was turned down by the state's only law school (the University of Oklahoma) because she was an African American. Backed by the NAACP, she took her case to the Supreme Court, which ruled that states must give black and white students equal educational opportunities. When she started classes, however, she was told to sit in a chair marked "colored" in a special roped-off section. Undeterred, she got her law degree in 1951, and some forty years later was invited to serve on the governing board of the University of Oklahoma.

In 1946 the YWCA finally ended its practice of separate branches for whites and blacks and began to integrate its programs.

Were any women leading scientists in the 1940s?

In 1947 Gerty Cori became the first American woman to win a Nobel Prize in science, in physiology and medicine. She and her husband, Carl, were awarded the prize jointly, for their work on glycogen metabolism—essentially, the way the body stores and breaks down sugar for use as energy. During the 1930s Gerty Cori had often been criticized for working with her husband and was even told it was un-American (she had been born abroad, in what is now Czechoslovakia). She was always given a lesser position than her husband and was not made a full professor until 1947, the year she won the Nobel Prize. The top U.S.

Another Nobel Peace Prize

In 1946 Emily Greene Balch became the second U.S. woman, after Jane Addams, to win the Nobel Peace Prize. Like Addams, she helped found the Women's International League for Peace and Freedom (WILPF). When Balch lost her teaching job at Wellesley College in 1919 because of her pacifist views, she put most of her energies into the peace movement.

As World War II approached, she spoke out against the attacks by the Japanese on the Chinese and by the Nazis on the Jews. She supported the U.S. war effort, but condemned the internment of Japanese Americans and urged the government to ease immigration restrictions for Jewish refugees. Balch gave most of her prize money to the WILPF.

Among the top choreographers, or creators of dance, in the 1940s were Martha Graham, Agnes de Mille, and Katherine Dunham.

scientific organization, the National Academy of Sciences, did not invite her to become a member until 1948, after she won the Nobel Prize.

What contributions did women make to theater and film in the 1940s?

In addition to actresses, there were several women, such as Lillian Hellman, who wrote Broadway plays, and a few women, such as Margo Jones and Antoinette Perry, who directed plays. When Perry died in 1946, the major New York theater awards—the Antoinette Perry Awards, nicknamed the Tony Awards—were established in her honor. A number of women wrote screenplays for Hollywood, but few were given directing jobs. Among the budding young film stars was 12-year-old Elizabeth Taylor played a young girl determined to ride in a horse race in *National Velvet* in 1944. In 1947 nine-year-old Natalie Wood captured many hearts in *Miracle on 34th Street*.

In 1931, at age 17, minor league player Jackie Mitchell pitched in an exhibition game against the New York Yankees. First, she struck out Babe Ruth; then, Lou Gehrig. Soon afterward, she was told that baseball was "too strenuous" for women and lost her minor league contract.

Who was the greatest woman athlete of the first half of the 20th century?

In 1950 the Associated Press called Babe Didrikson Zaharias the century's greatest woman athlete. Originally named Mildred, she earned the nickname "Babe" through a comparison to the great baseball star Babe Ruth. Zaharias was outstanding not just in baseball, but also in basketball, track and field, and golf. At the 1932 Olympics she won two gold medals and a silver in track and field events. Zaharias later helped start the Ladies Professional Golf Association and was the top money winner in women's golf for three straight years (1949-51).

THE PUSH FOR EQUAL RIGHTS (1950–80)

What was life like for women during the 1950s?

Throughout the 1950s public figures, the media, and above all advertising emphasized women's roles as mothers and homemakers. The ideal American woman was young, white, and middle class with a home in the suburbs, a hardworking husband, and at least two healthy children. She did not have a job outside the home; instead, her work was to care for her children and keep the house sparkling clean.

This ideal, however, was only an ideal. For most American women, life was very different. About a third of all women had jobs outside the home, including a fourth of all married women. Women were teachers, nurses, secretaries, salesclerks, factory workers, and domestics.

Were any women politicians in the 1950s?

A few women held important positions in politics in the 1950s. Most visible was Margaret Chase Smith, a Republican from Maine and the only woman in the U.S. Senate. In 1950 she gave a courageous speech denouncing Senator Joseph McCarthy and his growing witchhunt for anyone who expressed "un-American" beliefs or communist sympathies. Smith called on all senators to uphold such basic democratic principles as "the right to criticize; the right to hold unpopular beliefs; the right to protest; the right of independent thought." In the same year

In 1954 Democrats Edith Starrett Green of Oregon and Martha Wright Griffiths of Michigan were elected to the House of Representatives. Both helped write laws to improve women's rights.

In 1950 Mary Church Terrell, age 87, sued a restaurant in Washington, D.C., when it refused to serve her because she was African American. She won.

Representative Helen Gahagan Douglas of California, who had earlier issued a similar statement, was defeated in her race for a Senate seat when her opponent, Richard M. Nixon, attacked her as a communist sympathizer.

Several women served as ambassadors, most prominently Clare Boothe Luce as ambassador to Italy. In addition, Oveta Culp Hobby became the second woman cabinet officer, as secretary of health, education, and welfare under President Dwight David Eisenhower.

Who started the civil rights movement?

The actions of Rosa Parks in Montgomery, Alabama, in 1955 helped spark the civil rights movement. At the time African Americans traveling on local buses had to sit in a special section at the back, and if the bus filled up, they might be asked to give their seats to white passengers. On December 1, tired after a day of work, Parks took a seat with other African Americans in the back but soon was asked to give her seat to a white man. She refused and was promptly arrested.

When Parks, an active member of the local NAACP, agreed to fight her arrest in court, a black women's group, led by Jo Ann Robinson, organized a related protest against segregated seating on buses. Joined by the Reverend Martin Luther King, Jr., who became the leader of the new civil rights crusade, the women urged African Americans to stay off city buses on the day of Parks's trial. When Parks was found guilty, the boycott continued for more than a year. To avoid riding buses, many black women walked miles to their jobs. They kept the buses empty and made the boycott a success. Finally, in late 1956, the Supreme Court ruled that segregated seating on buses is illegal.

In 1955 Jean Blackwell Hutson took charge of the Schomburg Collection at the New York Library and helped create a major center for research on African American culture.

Did African American children have to go to separate schools in the 1950s?

In the early 1950s Linda Brown was told she could not attend a public school near her home in Topeka, Kansas, because she was black and the other students were white. Her parents sued and her case (*Brown v. Board of Education of Topeka*) led to the historic 1954 decision by the Supreme Court that separate schools for black and white children are unconstitutional because they are "inherently unequal."

How did African American women help integrate schools?

One of the most publicized integration efforts was organized by Daisy Lee Bates of the NAACP in 1957. Nine African American teenagers, six girls and three boys, made headlines when they integrated a high school in Little Rock, Arkansas, despite open resistance from the governor and attacks by white mobs. President Eisenhower sent federal troops to Little Rock to support the black students.

Other African Americans integrated state universities. In 1956 Autherine Lucy (later Foster) became the first black

On the first day Little Rock Central High School was integrated, September 4, 1957, Elizabeth Eckford walked to class in Little Rock, Arkansas, surrounded by anti-integrationists screaming racial epithets and protected by silent National Guardsmen.

In Washington State in 1961, when the government tried to restrict the fishing rights of the Nisqually people, Janet McCloud and other women protested by staging "fish-ins," taking the men's place in the boats when they were arrested.

student at the University of Alabama. But, after a white mob threw eggs and shouted at her, the school branded her a troublemaker and kicked her out. Nine years later, in 1965, Vivian Malone became that university's first black graduate. Charlayne Hunter (later Gault) was one of two black students to integrate the University of Georgia, in 1961. She later became a nationally known TV news reporter.

Were many African American women leaders in the civil rights movement?

Although African American women did not receive media attention as leaders, they played a major role in the civil rights movement. One of the most important was Ella Baker, who was in effect the executive director of Martin Luther King, Jr.'s organization, the Southern Christian Leadership Conference, in the late 1950s. She organized a major drive to register black voters and later advised the founders of the Student Nonviolent Coordinating Committee (SNCC) in 1960.

Ruby Doris Smith (later Robinson) and Diane Nash helped set up SNCC and participated in many sit-ins at public lunch counters in the South, refusing to leave when they were told African Americans would not be served.

Determined to Vote

In 1962 Fannie Lou Hamer, a farm-worker in Mississippi, became determined to pass the literacy test southern states used to keep black citizens from voting. As a result, she was fired from her job, lost her home, and was shot at—but she did pass the test and began teaching others how to pass it. Determined, as she put it, "to bring in justice where we've had so much injustice," she joined many civil

rights demonstrations and was severely beaten at one point. In 1964 she and other activists challenged the all-white delegation representing Mississippi at the Democratic Party's national convention. Her speech there was televised, and she convinced many Americans to support the civil rights movement with her description of the beatings she and others had received while fighting for basic rights.

Fannie Lou Hamer, a Mississippi farm laborer, worked to regain the African American right to vote in the South.

Did President John F. Kennedy do anything for women?

Soon after he became president, Kennedy set up the Presidential Commission on the Status of Women, chaired by former first lady Eleanor Roosevelt. In its 1963 report this commission called for a variety of reforms, including equal pay for similar work, child-care services, and protection against long hours and low pay for agricultural workers and domestics.

How did the civil rights movement affect women?

The civil rights struggle helped spark the women's movement of the later 1960s and early 1970s, just as the abolitionist movement energized the 19th-century women's movement. More directly, the Civil Rights Act of 1964 had a major impact on women's rights. One part of this law

In 1963 four African American schoolgirls were killed when whites bombed a black church in Birmingham, Alabama. These murders outraged many Americans.

Patsy Mink of Hawaii became the first Japanese American woman elected to Congress, in 1964.

prohibited job discrimination on the basis of race, religion, national origin, or sex. With this provision, women had an important weapon for fighting against discriminatory hiring and firing practices. By 1966 they had filed 4,000 complaints with the Equal Employment Opportunity Commission (EEOC), an agency set up to review violations of the law.

How did the National Organization for Women (NOW) begin?

At a 1966 national conference on women's status, some participants expressed their frustration that little had been done to enforce the 1964 Civil Rights Act's ban on sex discrimination in employment. When the conference leaders refused to demand action on this issue, Betty Friedan and others angrily gathered together and sketched out plans for a new organization for women's rights—**NOW.** The group's statement of purpose, written primarily by civil

Betty Friedan, cofounder of the National Organization for Women, holds up buttons at NOW's 1970 fourth anniversary meeting. NOW had 4,000 members at that point.

The Feminine Mystique

In 1963 Betty Friedan published her book *The Feminine Mystique,* which attacked the popular notion that women should aim to be perfect mothers and housewives as their highest achievement. She argued, "We can no longer ignore that voice within women that says: 'I want something more than my husband and my children and my home.'" Many women, especially middle-class women living in the suburbs, responded to Friedan's message, and her book quickly became a best-seller. Friedan soon found herself at the center of a new women's movement.

rights lawyer Pauli Murray, underlined that "the time has come to confront, with concrete action, the conditions that now prevent women from enjoying the equality of opportunity and freedom . . . which is their right, as individual Americans, and as human beings." Friedan served as NOW's first president.

What was the women's liberation movement?

In 1967–68 a group of young women started the **women's liberation movement,** a radical feminist movement, distinct from NOW. These women demanded freedom from "oppression" by men. A much publicized event was a 1968 demonstration against the Miss America Pageant at which women threw bras, curlers, high heels, and similar "garbage" into a "Freedom Trash Can." More typically, however, women met in small groups, known as *consciousness-raising (CR) groups,* to talk about their personal experiences and how to use those experiences as the basis for political action. "The personal is political" became a popular cry of the movement.

Were women active in the peace movement in the 1960s?

In the early 1960s several women were leaders in the call for a ban on nuclear weapons. In 1961, for example, a group called Women Strike for Peace staged a one-day walkout by 50,000 women. "End the arms race—not the human race" was their motto. Later, in the mid-1960s, thousands of women joined men in demonstrations against the Vietnam War.

Folksinger Joan Baez, whose songs strongly opposed the Vietnam War, made headlines when she was arrested in 1967 for protesting the draft.

Upstaging a Congressional Committee

In 1962 a committee of the House of Representatives decided to question Women Strike for Peace about supposed "un-American activities." But the committee was not prepared for the response. Every time a woman was called to testify, all the women in the room stood up or clapped to support her. One woman clearly pointed out that the group was started, not by radicals who were trying to overthrow the government, but by mothers who loved their children. When another woman was asked if Communists could join the group, she answered, "Unless everybody in the world joins us in this fight, then God help us." The House committee soon called off the investigation.

About 10,000 women served in the military forces in the Vietnam War, which ended in 1973. Most were nurses.

Did any women serve as civil rights leaders in the late 1960s?

Coretta Scott King emerged as an important figure in the civil rights movement after her husband, Martin Luther King, Jr., was assassinated in 1968. She helped organize a 1968 march of poor people in Washington, D.C., and participated in many other demonstrations. She also set up the Martin Luther King, Jr., Center for Nonviolent Social Change.

Were any African American women in Congress in the late 1960s?

Shirley Chisholm of Brooklyn, New York, was the first African American woman elected to the House of Representatives, in 1968. In her autobiography Unbought and Unbossed, she credited "womanpower" with her victory.

In 1972 Chisholm became the first African American to run for president in the Democratic primaries. She said she wanted "to open the way for women to think that they can run," but many women's groups did not back her candidacy.

The National Conference of Puerto Rican Women was started in 1972.

Were Mexican American women active in the early women's movement?

A number of Chicanas formed their own women's rights organizations in the early 1970s, within the context of the broader Mexican American civil rights struggle. The first national conference of Chicanas was held in Houston, Texas, in 1971. In 1974 the Mexican American Women's National Association (MANA) was formed. The group protested the practice of sterilizing Mexican American women without their consent, which meant they could no longer bear children.

Did Native American women form feminist groups in the 1970s?

Many Native American women focused on their own peoples' struggles. LaDonna Harris set up the national group Americans for Indian Opportunity in 1970; Ada Deer helped lead the Menominees' fight to be recognized by the federal government as a distinct people, entitled to their tribal lands and health and education benefits; and Ramona Bennett lobbied for recognition of the Puyallup people. Other women were active in the American Indian Movement, and AIM activists Lorelei Means and Madonna Thunderhawk helped start Women of All Red Nations (WARN) in 1974.

How prominent were African American women in the new women's movement?

African American women such as Aileen Hernandez and Pauli Murray were early leaders in NOW. When Hernandez was elected as NOW's second president, after Betty Friedan, she said, "As a black woman, I particularly

The Organization of Pan-Asian American Women was started in 1976 to coordinate the work of groups of women of Asian and Pacific Islander descent.

"Free Angela"

In 1970 African American activist Angela Davis, a college professor, became a symbol of defiance for many young radicals. She was accused of supplying a gun for a deadly courtroom shootout after an African American prisoner she had defended was killed. When she fled arrest, the FBI put her on the "10 Most Wanted" list. Later, after she was caught and charged with murder, many people protested, arguing that she was innocent. "Free Angela" T-shirts and bumper stickers spread across the country. After more than a year in jail, Davis was tried and found not guilty.

In 1972 congress-women Bella Abzug and Shirley Chisholm, feminists Betty Friedan and Gloria Steinem, and others formed the National Women's Political Caucus to push for more political representation for women.

think that it is important to be involved in women's liberation."

African American feminists started the National Black Feminist Organization in 1973. Another black feminist group, the Combahee River Collective in Boston, issued a statement in 1977 urging African American women to organize.

Did women hold any large demonstrations for their rights in the 1970s?

On August 26, 1970, the 50th anniversary of women's suffrage, NOW sponsored Women's Strike for Equality, with demonstrations across the country. In New York about 50,000 women marched down Fifth Avenue to call for an end to the discrimination women still faced.

How did women try to gain equal rights in the 1970s?

A major focus of the women's movement in the 1970s was on passage of the Equal Rights Amendment (ERA), which stated, "Equality of rights under the law shall not   be denied . . . on account of sex." In 1972, after the House and the Senate passed the ERA, it went to the states for approval. Although twenty-one states approved it in 1972, it failed to get approval from the necessary thirty-eighty states within the time frame allowed. Three more votes were needed when the deadline expired in 1982.

Why did feminists want an Equal Rights Amendment?

In her autobiography, Congresswoman Bella Abzug summarized the two main benefits of the ERA: "First, laws that confer benefits of one kind or another will be extended to both sexes. . . . Second, laws that restrict opportunities would be declared unconstitutional." Abzug mentioned, for example, that at the time many married women could not get credit on their own because all property was in the husband's name. Also, women could not get certain jobs because they were not allowed to lift heavy weights or work overtime.

Who opposed the Equal Rights Amendment?

One of the most vocal and effective opponents of the ERA was Phyllis Schlafly, who quickly set up the National Committee to Stop ERA in 1972. She portrayed feminism and the ERA as "a total assault on the role of the American woman as a wife and mother, and on the family as the basic unit of society." Anti-feminists argued that the ERA would force women to fight in wars and lead to unisex public toilets, among other things.

What breakthroughs did women in government make in the 1970s?

In 1974 in Connecticut, Ella Grasso became the first woman to be elected governor in her own right, not as a successor to her husband.

In 1976 Representative Barbara Jordan of Texas became the first woman and the first African American to give the main speech at the Democratic National Convention. This honor, she said, "is one additional bit of evidence that the American Dream need not forever be deferred."

In 1977 President Jimmy Carter appointed two women to his cabinet. Patricia Roberts Harris became the first African American woman in a cabinet position,

In 1975 the Supreme Court ruled that women had to be routinely called for jury duty just as men were. Until this decision, Louisiana women who wanted to serve on juries had to request for the chance in writing.

Chicana Labor Activists

Mexican American women's contribution to the success of labor struggles can be seen in the movie *Salt of the Earth*, which is based on a 1951 strike by Chicano miners in New Mexico. When the men were forbidden to walk the picket lines, the women took over and were not stopped by tear gas or arrests. The strikers eventually won.

Since the early 1960s, the most visible Chicana labor leader has been Dolores Huerta, who helped César Chávez start the United Farm Workers in 1962. In 1968–69 she helped organize a major national boycott of grapes, which led to better pay and working conditions for the grape pickers. Even though she was brutally beaten by police and almost lost her life, she continued to fight for farm workers—recently with a 1997 crusade to help strawberry pickers in California.

as secretary of housing and urban development, and Juanita Kreps became the first woman secretary of commerce.

Were there any large women's meetings in the 1970s?

In connection with the UN International Women's Year, the U.S. government sponsored a National Women's Conference in Houston, Texas, in 1977. Some 20,000 women participated in this event. The group called for passage of the Equal Rights Amendment and voiced its commitment to the rights of both people of color and lesbians. As a symbolic gesture, a lighted torch was passed woman to woman from Seneca Falls in New York to Houston, a distance of 2,600 miles.

What gains did working women make in the 1960s and 1970s?

Backed by the 1964 Civil Rights Act, which made job discrimination illegal, women ended a variety of unfair employment practices. "Help Wanted" listings could no longer be separated into jobs for men only or women only—unless there was a valid reason for this division. Stewardesses could no longer be forced to retire if they married or reached age 32. Magazines such as *Newsweek* and newspapers such as the *New York Times* were compelled to revise hiring and promotion policies that left women in the lowest-paid positions. Companies such as AT&T, which employed thousands of women, had to give millions of dollars in back pay to women who had been treated unfairly. Even leading universities faced lawsuits if they did not give women an equal chance to become professors.

Women's relative pay dropped from 60 cents for every dollar a man earned in 1960 to 59 cents in 1970. Women of color typically earned even less.

What kinds of new jobs opened for women in the 1970s?

In the 1970s for the first time women became FBI agents, jet pilots for major airlines, and steelworkers. Despite these and other breakthroughs, there were still relatively few women in top executive positions.

Did women start their own businesses in the 1960s and 1970s?

One of the most successful new businesswomen of the 1960s was Mary Kay Ash, who started Mary Kay Cosmetics and encouraged other women to set up businesses by selling her products. Muriel Siebert set up her own stock brokerage firm in 1967 and later became the first woman to buy a seat on the New York Stock Exchange.

In the 1970s women opened their own stores, restaurants, advertising agencies, computer companies, food-manufacturing companies, and much more. Most visible were women fashion designers with their own clothing lines, including Diane Von Furstenberg, Carole Little, Elisabeth Claiborne Ortenberg, and Josie Cruz Natori.

Did any new laws help working women during the 1960s and 1970s?

In addition to the 1964 Civil Rights Act, Congress passed the Equal Pay Act in 1963. This act required equal pay for equal work—although it did not include all jobs. The law was extended to cover executives and professionals in 1972, but it still did not help the many women who were domestics and agricultural workers. In 1974 Congress finally said domestic workers had to be paid the minimum wage, more than twenty-five years after factory workers won this right. A 1978 law banned job discrimination against pregnant women.

Were there major strikes by women in the 1960s and 1970s?

Following a 1959 strike in New York, hospital workers (mostly women) began to organize successfully. In 1969 hospital workers in Charleston, South Carolina, walked off their jobs for 113 days and gained recognition for their union. "We 400 hospital workers—almost all of us women, and all of us black—were compelled to go on strike so that we could win the right to be treated as human beings," organizer Mary Ann Moultrie explained. Civil rights leaders such as Coretta Scott King supported the workers.

Office Workers Revolt

Women office workers began to organize in the 1970s, forming such groups as Women Employed in Chicago, Women Office Workers in New York, and 9 to 5 in Boston. By 1976 there was a national organization, Working Women, to fight for better pay and conditions for office workers. In 1977 secretary Iris Rivera made headlines when she refused to make coffee for her male boss. She declared, "(1) I don't drink coffee, (2) it's not listed as one of my job duties, and (3) ordering the secretary to fix the coffee is carrying the role of homemaker too far." When she was fired for her revolt, a number of secretaries staged a protest in Chicago's business district, Women Employed leant its support, and she soon got her job back.

Did women workers from different industries ever combine their efforts?

In 1974 women from fifty-eight unions joined forces in the Coalition of Labor Union Women (CLUW). They were determined to fight against sexism within national unions, improve women's working conditions, and organize the 30 million women workers who did not belong to unions.

What opportunities were there for women teachers in the 1960s and 1970s?

Although many women were teachers, only a few held the top positions. Especially at the university level, women were much less likely than men to get the top teaching jobs. At the Harvard Graduate School of Arts and Sciences, for example, only 1 woman was a tenured professor compared with 410 men in 1970. In the public schools, more than 80 percent of the principals were men in 1970. Few women headed colleges or universities; in fact, Smith College, one of the early women's colleges, named its first woman president only in 1975, after it had been open for 100 years.

Yale and Princeton opened their doors to women undergraduates in 1969 and 1970, respectively.

When did women's studies start?

The first women's studies courses were offered at San Diego State College in 1969; by 1974 there were complete

The Rights of Women on Welfare

In the late 1960s Chicana and African American women formed welfare rights organizations. The largest group was the National Welfare Rights Organization (NWRO), with 22,000 members in 1969. It not only helped women get the benefits they were entitled to, but also lobbied for job training, day-care facilities, and, above all, respect for the work in the home women always did.

As Johnnie Tillmon, head of the NWRO, put it, "If I were president . . . I'd start paying women a living wage for doing the work we are already doing—child-raising and housekeeping."

women's studies programs at more than eighty colleges. A few public elementary and high schools began teaching special courses on women in 1971.

In 1978 for the first time more women enrolled in college than men.

Did education for women improve in the 1970s?

In 1972 Congress passed an important law. Known as **Title IX**, this law prohibits sex discrimination in any school that receives funds from the federal government. A major, unforeseen effect was to boost sports programs for girls. Another law, the Women's Education Equity Act of 1974, provided money for the development of nonsexist teaching materials.

When did women become ministers in major Protestant denominations?

In the mid-1950s women began to be ordained as Presbyterian ministers and Methodist women ministers gained equal status with men. Lutheran women first became ministers in 1970. The Episcopal Church officially approved female priests in 1976 after eleven women were unofficially ordained in a Philadelphia ceremony in 1974.

Was there a women's movement in religion?

In the early 1970s a number of women began reexamining women's spirituality and offering a feminist view of religion. In particular, some feminists explored

Women rabbis were first allowed in Reform Judaism in 1972.

Standing Up for Children

In 1973 Marian Wright Edelman formed the Children's Defense Fund to bring children's rights and needs to public attention. She wrote that she did this because she had "learned that critical civil and political rights would not mean much to a hungry, homeless, illiterate child and family if they lacked the social and economic means to exercise them."

ancient peoples' worship of goddesses and developed new rituals and ceremonies to celebrate the female Goddess rather than the male God of traditional Christianity.

How did the women's movement affect health care?

With the women's movement, an increasing number of women wanted to take charge of their own health care and make informed decisions about medical treatments. In 1970 the Boston Women's Health Book Collective published *Our Bodies, Ourselves* to give women information on sex, childbearing, and other health concerns—information that was often unavailable from doctors at the time. Also in the early 1970s, women started their own health clinics to provide information and offer care, especially to low-income women. By 1976 the National

In 1978 Faye Wattleton became both the first woman and the first African American president of Planned Parenthood, the organization started by Margaret Sanger.

Ending Violence Against Women

The women's movement helped focus attention on the need to end violent attacks against women and to help women and children who suffered from these attacks. One woman, whose husband had held a gun to her head for hours, said, "What is needed first and foremost are emergency aid shelters to provide comprehensive services to women and children." During the 1970s women all over the United States set up rape crisis centers, battered women's shelters, and groups to publicize the issue of **domestic violence**. In 1978 women started "Take Back the Night" marches to assert their right to walk at night on city streets without fear of being attacked.

Women's Health Network was formed in Washington, D.C., as a general clearinghouse for information on women's health care issues.

In 1960 the U.S. government approved the first birth control pill, giving women more choice over when to have children.

When did abortion become a major national issue?

In the 1950s and 1960s **abortion,** deliberately ending a pregnancy, was a crime in most states, even for a woman whose life was in danger. If a woman wanted a safe abortion, she had to go abroad. In desperation some women had illegal abortions, and a number died as a result.

In the 1960s women began to lobby for the reform of abortion laws, and by 1970 a few states allowed women to get legal abortions. A major change came in 1973 when, in *Roe v. Wade*, the Supreme Court ruled that women should be able to choose to have an abortion during the first several months of pregnancy. This decision invalidated the laws in forty-six states (all but Alaska, Hawaii, New York, and Washington).

After the Supreme Court ruling, abortion became a hot political issue. Congress voted not to pay for abortions for women receiving government medical aid. From the late 1970s on, different states passed laws setting conditions for obtaining an abortion, such as the requirement that teenage girls get their parents' consent. The Supreme Court upheld many of these laws.

When did people begin to worry about the environment?

In many ways, the environmental movement was sparked by biologist Rachel Carson's book *Silent Spring* (1962). She exposed how the increasing use of pesticides was killing birds, silencing the birdsongs that traditionally announced spring, and harming humans.

How many women were scientists in the 1960s?

By 1960 more than a fourth of all U.S. biologists and mathematicians were women, but less than a tenth of all chemists and less then a twentieth of all physicists were women. Only 1 percent of engineers were women.

Cleaning Up the Waste

In the late 1970s Lois Gibbs, a homemaker in upstate New York, became concerned by the health problems in her community, built around a waterway called Love Canal. She traced the illnesses and birth defects, as well as the strong smells, to pollution from a toxic waste dump. She then organized other women in the area, got the national media alarmed about the problem, and successfully forced government agencies to start cleaning up the dump. Afterward she started the Citizen's Clearinghouse for Hazardous Wastes to teach other communities how to organize in similar situations.

Did any U.S. women scientists win the Nobel Prize between 1950 and 1980?

In 1963 Marie Goeppert Mayer received the Nobel Prize in physics for her work on the structure of atoms. Although she did not win the Nobel Prize, physicist Chien-Shiung Wu also made important discoveries about atomic particles, which supported the work of two male colleagues who won the Nobel Prize in 1957.

In 1977 physicist Rosalyn Yalow was awarded the Nobel Prize in physiology or medicine for her work in developing radioimmunoassay, a technique used to diagnose diabetes, thyroid disease, and other medical problems. In her acceptance speech she pointed to the need to improve opportunities for women scientists: "The world cannot afford the loss of the talents of half its people."

What happened to women in the military in the 1960s and 1970s?

In 1967 a new law ended the limit on the top rank women officers could achieve. As a result, women began to be promoted to the positions of general and rear admiral in the 1970s. The 1967 law also did away with the 2 percent limit on the number of women in the services.

In 1975 Congress opened West Point, Annapolis, and the other military academies to women. Also in 1975, married women with children were allowed to serve in the mil-

Jacqueline Cochran, who helped organize women pilots during World War II, was the first woman pilot to break the sound barrier, in 1953.

One of the female cadets at West Point, the U.S. military academy, graduates.

itary for the first time. In 1978 women obtained the right to serve on noncombat ships in the navy.

Were many women television news reporters in the 1960s and 1970s?

The first national TV news correspondent was Nancy Dickerson, hired by CBS in 1960. However, not many women reporters were seen on TV until the 1970s, when the Federal Communications Commission made stations adopt plans to hire more women. A few women became coanchors on local evening news programs, and in 1976 ABC signed Barbara Walters as the first woman coanchor

Ms. magazine, edited by Gloria Steinem, first came out in 1972; it soon had 350,000 readers.

In the 1970s women started their own publishing houses, such as the Feminist Press.

on a national evening news program. Walters left that program in 1978 and in 1979 began cohosting the TV show *20/20*.

Did many women write poetry between 1950 and 1980?

Hundreds of women published poetry during this period. Gwendolyn Brooks became the first African American woman to win the Pulitzer Prize in poetry, in 1950, with *Annie Allen*. Marianne Moore was the first woman to win another top poetry honor, the Bollingen Prize, in 1952. In the 1960s and 1970s Sylvia Plath and Anne Sexton were known for very personal poems about their emotional struggles; both committed suicide.

Who were some other writers in the 1960s and 1970s?

Such well-known and top-selling contemporary novelists as Anne Tyler, Joyce Carol Oates, Anne Rice, Toni Morrison, and Alice Walker published their first books in the 1960s and 1970s. In addition to novels, there were powerful autobiographical stories, such as *I Know Why the Caged Bird Sings* by Maya Angelou and *The Woman Warrior: Memoirs of a Girlhood among Ghosts* by Maxine Hong Kingston.

Were there any breakthroughs for women playwrights between 1950 and 1980?

In 1959 Lorraine Hansberry became the first African American woman to have a play staged on Broadway—*A Raisin in the Sun*, about what happens when a black family's dreams are postponed. But it was 1976 before another play by an African American woman made it to Broadway: Ntozake Shange's smash hit *For colored girls who have considered suicide/when the rainbow is enuf*.

Miriam Colón started the Puerto Rican Traveling Theater in New York in 1967, and Tisa Chang set up the Pan Asian Repertory Theater in New York in 1977.

Did new opportunities open up for women in music in the 1960s and 1970s?

A growing number of women got recording contracts and concert dates after 1960, and women were among the top performers in almost every kind of music. Women

Playwright Lorraine Hansberry's 1959 hit *A Raisin in the Sun* moved from Broadway to the big screen in 1961. The movie's stars included Sidney Poitier, left, Claudia McNeil, center, and Ruby Dee, right.

gained increasing visibility in major orchestras, and in 1976 Sarah Caldwell became the first woman to conduct the Metropolitan Opera. The year before, Caldwell had conducted the New York Philharmonic in a program of works by women composers.

Feminism in the Art World

In the 1970s women artists began protesting their lack of representation in major museum shows and galleries. They also started their own cooperative galleries. Miriam Schapiro and Judy Chicago started a feminist art program in Los Angeles. Chicago later worked with other women to create *The Dinner Party* (1979), a huge table with specially designed place settings honoring thirty-nine famous women. In 1976 art historians Ann Sutherland Harris and Linda Nochlin demonstrated that there were many great women artists in the past with a major traveling exhibit, *Women Artists 1550–1950*. A similar show on American women architects was put together by Susanna Torre in 1977.

Changes in Tennis

Althea Gibson changed the world of tennis in 1950 when she became the first African American, male or female, to play at the U.S. Open, the national championships. Then, in 1957, she became the first black player to win the singles championship at Wimbledon in England. She was honored with a ticker-tape parade on her return. Also in 1957, Gibson became the first African American to win the singles at the U.S. Open.

Billie Jean King, who won the first of six Wimbledon singles championships in 1967, also changed the tennis world. She called attention to the big difference in the prize money for male and female champions. Her efforts led the U.S. Open to equalize its prizes in 1973. Also in 1973, King won a much publicized "Battle of the Sexes," defeating the 1939 male Wimbledon champion, Bobby Riggs, in three easy sets.

Janet Guthrie was the first female racer in the Indianapolis 500; in 1977, she finished in eighth place in 1978.

How did the women's movement affect women filmmakers?

In the 1970s many women began making their own, independent films. One example was *Girlfriends*, directed by Claudia Weill, which was highly praised by the critics. Women also set up their own film distribution companies, such as Women Make Movies.

Billie Jean King, winner of six women's tennis Wimbledon titles, was one of the greatest female athletes of all time, as well as an outspoken supporter of equality for women tennis players.

Did women gain new positions in the federal government in the 1980s? ◆ Who were the first women appointed to the Supreme Court? ◆ Were there any women in the U.S. Senate in the 1980s? ◆ What was the highest number of women in the House of Representatives during the 1980s? ◆ Why was Geraldine Ferraro important? ◆ How many women ran for office in the early 1990s? ◆ How many women were elected to the House of Representatives in the early 1990s? ◆ Did the number of women in the U.S. Senate increase in the early 1990s? ◆ Have many women won election as governor since 1980? ◆ Has

New Roles for Women (1980–Present)

Did women gain new positions in the federal government in the 1980s?

In 1981 Jeane Kirkpatrick became the first permanent U.S. woman ambassador to the United Nations. She later said she "realized that not only was I the first woman ever to represent the United States . . . I was the first woman to represent any major power."

Several women served in the cabinet during the 1980s, including Elizabeth Dole, first as secretary of transportation and later as secretary of labor. Antonia Novello became the first woman and first Latina to serve as U.S. surgeon-general, in 1989.

Who were the first women appointed to the Supreme Court?

In 1981 Sandra Day O'Connor became the first woman appointed to the U.S. Supreme Court. At that time less than 6 percent of all federal judges were women. In 1993 Ruth Bader Ginsburg became the second woman on the Supreme Court. In her acceptance speech, she said that her nomination "contributes to the end of the days when women, at least half the talent pool of our society, appear in high places only as one-at-a-time performers."

In 1989 Judith Chang Bloch became the first Asian American woman ambas-sador, to Nepal.

A Major Native American Chief

In 1985 Wilma Mankiller became the first woman principal chief of the Cherokee Nation in Oklahoma; she served in this position until 1994. Mankiller focused on increasing job and educational opportunities for the Cherokee people. In 1990 she signed an important agreement giving the Cherokee Nation control over the federal funds it received and greater power to govern itself. Her approval rating was so high that she won her reelection in 1991 by a landslide, with 83 percent of the vote. Later, in her autobiography, she wrote, "Prior to my becoming chief, young Cherokee girls never thought they might be able to grow up and become chief themselves. That has definitely changed."

Ileana Ros-Lehtinen of Florida became the first Cuban American elected to the U.S. House of Representatives, in 1989.

Were there any women in the U.S. Senate in the 1980s?

In the early 1980s there was only one woman senator, Nancy Kassebaum of Kansas. In 1987 she was joined by Barbara Mikulski, the first woman senator from Maryland.

What was the highest number of women in the House of Representatives during the 1980s?

In 1989 there were twenty-six women representatives, the highest number ever. There were still, however, more than sixteen times as many men.

Why was Geraldine Ferraro important?

In 1984 Democratic presidential candidate Walter Mondale named Representative Geraldine Ferraro from Queens, New York, as his running mate. She was the first woman to be nominated as a vice presidential candidate for one of the main political parties. After the Mondale-Ferraro ticket lost, Ferraro wrote a book about her experience. She said she wanted people to vote for her "because they thought I would make the best Vice President." But she also said that "I ran as a woman, and brought a different perspective."

In 1985 Ellen Malcolm founded EMILY's List, a group that raises money for Democratic women who support women's rights and run for political office. The acronym EMILY stands for Early Money Is Like Yeast.

Did many women run for office in the early 1990s?

For the 1992 election women's groups focused on increasing the number of women running for office—

What Angered Women

In 1991 national attention focused on the two different stories told by Clarence Thomas, then a nominee for the Supreme Court, and Anita Hill, a lawyer who had worked for him ten years earlier. Hill claimed Thomas had sexually harassed her, making her uncomfortable with his remarks and behavior. Many women were angered when members of the all-male Senate Judiciary Committee attacked Hill's character, putting her on trial, so to speak. Thomas, who denied Hill's charges, was appointed to the Supreme Court, but many people believed that Hill had spoken the truth. Women began to speak out more forcefully about the problem of **sexual harassment.** They also worked to elect more women to political office and to get at least one woman on the Senate Judiciary Committee.

and winning. NOW, for example, organized an "Elect Women for a Change" campaign. More women ran for office than in any previous election, and more women won.

How many women were elected to the House of Representatives in the early 1990s?

With the 1992 election the number of women representatives almost doubled, rising to forty-eight. Lucille Roybal-Allard of California became the first Mexican American and Nydia Velázquez of New York the first Puerto Rican congresswoman.

Did the number of women in the U.S. Senate increase in the early 1990s?

The 1992 election tripled the number of women in the Senate, from two to six. California became the first state to have two women senators: Dianne Feinstein and Barbara Boxer. Illinois elected the first African American woman senator: Carol Moseley-Braun. And Washington voted in its first woman senator: Patty Murray. Later in 1993, Kay Hutchinson won a special election in Texas, bringing the total number of women in the Senate to seven.

Have many women won election as governor since 1980?

More women have been elected governor in the 1980s and 1990s than in the previous sixty years combined. Among the new states to gain women governors were Kansas (Joan Finney), Kentucky (Martha Layne Collins), Nebraska (Kay Orr), New Hampshire (Jeanne Shaheen), New Jersey (Christine Todd Whitman), and Vermont (Madeleine Kunin). Ann Richards became the second woman governor of Texas in 1990.

Has the number of women mayors in major cities increased since 1980?

In recent years more women have been elected mayor in large cities than ever before. In 1989 the four largest Texas cities—El Paso, Dallas, Houston, and San Antonio—all had women mayors. In 1990 Washington, D.C., gained its first woman mayor—Sharon Pratt Dixon (later Kelly), also the first black woman to head one of the top 20 American cities. By 1993 the second and third largest California cities—San Diego and San Jose—had women mayors.

Have women been appointed to important positions in President Bill Clinton's administration?

More women have been named to key jobs in President Clinton's administration than in any previous administration. In 1997 Madeleine Albright, who had served as ambassador to the United Nations, became the first woman secretary of state, assuming the highest cabinet position. Earlier, in 1993, Janet Reno became the first woman attorney general, Hazel O'Leary the first woman and first African American secretary of energy, and Jocelyn Elders the first African American woman surgeon general. Women have also held many other influential positions, including secretary of health and human services (Donna Shalala), secretary of labor (Alexis Herman), head of the Environmental Protection Agency (Carol Browner), chair of the Council of Economic Advisors (Laura Tyson), director of the Office of Management and Budget (Alice Rivlin), secretary of the Air Force (Sheila Widnall), and press secretary (Dee Dee Myers).

In 1997 hundreds of thousands of African American women joined the Million Woman March in Philadelphia to celebrate sisterhood and encourage community involvement.

Future Goals

Although the number of women in elected office has greatly increased in recent years, there are still far fewer women than men in the top positions. When will there be a woman president or vice president, and when will the number of women in Congress equal the number of men? In 1997 there were about ten times as many men in the House of Representatives as women, and about twelve times as many men as women in the Senate. In fact, most states had never had even one woman senator. More than three-fourths of the states had yet to elect a woman governor in 1997, and many cities had never had a woman mayor. More and more women, however, are now running for office, so women can be expected to achieve many more firsts in politics.

Have any new laws helped women since 1980?

New laws have made it easier for widows and divorced women to collect retirement benefits and for divorced mothers who are raising their children to collect child support from their ex-husbands. Other laws have strengthened the provisions against discrimination in education or employment, provided funding for battered women's shelters, and increased services for victims of rape and domestic violence.

Did women do much to help their communities in the 1980s and 1990s?

All over the United States, thousands of women have set up local programs to improve people's lives. Two examples are Kathy Levin, who started Magic Me in Baltimore, a program through which children living in the inner city gained self-confidence by helping people in old-age homes, and Rita Zimmer, who set up Women in Need in New York City, an organization that runs a shelter for homeless women, a food canteen, and day-care services.

Have women been active in the environmental movement since 1980?

Starting in the 1980s women held meetings on ecofeminism to discuss the relation between ecology,

Candy Lightner founded Mothers Against Drunk Driving (MADD) in 1980, after her daughter was killed by a drunk driver.

In 1994 muralists Juana Alicia, Miranda Bergman, Edythe Boone, Susan Kelk Cervantes, Meera Desai, Yvonne Littleton, and Irene Perez painted the outside of the Women's Building in San Francisco with inspiring images of women. According to its mission statement, "the Women's Building is a neighborhood and women's center committed to providing the tools, resources and information for women and girls to reach their full potential and participate equally in the governance of their lives and their communities."

feminism, and women's spirituality. Female environmental scientists, like Jessica Tuchman Mathews at the World Resources Institute, spoke out against air pollution and global warming. Native American women protested against industrial developments that threatened their peoples' lands: Sarah James, for example, organized the Gwich'in people to fight against oil and gas companies' plans for the Alaska coastal plain. In California in the 1990s activist Judy Bari helped lead demonstrations to save the redwood forests.

Did most women have jobs in the 1980s and 1990s?

By 1980 more than half of all women had jobs outside the home, and by the mid-1990s women represented almost half of all workers. In 1994 the U.S. Census Bureau predicted that 99 percent of all U.S. women would work for pay at some point in their lives.

The Glass Ceiling

The **glass ceiling** is an invisible barrier that prevents women and people of color from rising to top positions in corporations. In 1991 the government set up a special commission to examine the glass ceiling. In 1995 this commission reported that white men held 95 percent of all top management positions.

Did women earn as much as men in the mid-1990s?

By the mid-1990s women were earning slightly more than 70 cents for every dollar earned by men, compared with less than 60 cents in the early 1970s. For women with Ph.D.s the rate was higher, but still less than 80 percent of what men earned.

Is sexual harassment on the job legal?

In 1986 the Supreme Court ruled that sexual harassment is a form of sex discrimination and, because of that, is against the law. In 1992 the Supreme Court said that sexual harassment of students is also illegal.

Have many women become business owners in recent years?

By 1987 women owned more than a quarter of all U.S. businesses; by 1992 this number had risen to a third. Part of

The Woman at the Helm

In the early 1990s Katharine Graham stepped down as the head of the Washington Post Company after thirty years. As the owner of both the *Washington Post* and *Newsweek*, she had been one of the most influential people in the news business. Yet in her 1997 autobiography she reflected, "I always thought things would grow better with time, that the atmosphere [at the top] would become more welcoming of women . . . but it didn't happen that way. For one thing, there never were that many more of us— and still aren't, at least not at the highest levels."

Many women have become priests since 1980, and some have been ordained as some bishops in Protestant churches.

this increase was due to the Women's Business Ownership Act of 1988, which eased restrictions that had made it difficult for many women to apply for commercial credit.

When was the first Take Our Daughters to Work Day?

The Ms. Foundation for Women sponsored the first Take Our Daughters to Work Day in 1993 in the hopes of showing girls the variety of jobs women can do.

Has girls' education changed since 1980?

Educators have developed many books and teaching materials on women's history in the years since 1980. Special emphasis has been placed on interesting girls in math and science. In the mid-1990s Congress voted specifically to provide money to promote math and science education for girls. It also supported programs to improve teachers' sensitivity to girls' educational needs.

Did any women start new colleges since 1980?

In 1982 Jeanine Pease-Windy Boy opened Little Big Horn College in an old house and two trailers in Montana. By the early 1990s more than 300 residents of the Crow Reservation were attending its classes each year. Often the classes were taught in the Crow language.

Women's History Month

Each March the country celebrates Women's History Month. The idea for this national event came from the National Women's History Research Project, which was founded in California in 1980 to encourage the study of women's history in all school grades, from kindergarten up. The resolution passed by Congress for Women's History Month underlines women's contribution to U.S. history by stating, "American women of every race, class, and ethnic background have made historic contributions to the growth of our Nation in countless recorded and unrecorded ways."

When did the first woman astronaut go into space?

In 1983, after about five years of training, physicist Sally Ride became the first woman in space. She has been followed by a number of other women, including Mae Jemison, the first African American woman in space (1992), and Ellen Ochoa, the first Latina in space (1993). In 1995 Eileen Collins became the first woman astronaut to pilot a spacecraft. In 1997 Shannon Lucid set a record for the longest time spent in space by any U.S. astronaut—more than six months.

Astronaut Sally Ride displays her tool kit on the space shuttle before taking off to become the first U.S. woman in space in 1983.

In the 1980s and 1990s the National Academy of Sciences admitted more women than in all the other years combined since its founding in 1863.

Have any U.S. women scientists won the Nobel Prize since 1980?

Three women won the Nobel Prize in physiology or medicine in the 1980s: Barbara McClintock in 1983 for work on genes, Rita Levi-Montalcini in 1986 for work on the growth of nerve cells, and Gertrude Elion in 1988 for developing several new drugs, including one used in heart transplants.

Have there been any recent advances in women's health care?

Since 1980 women have started a number of health information groups, such as the National Black Women's Health Project and the National Latina Health Organization. In the 1990s Congress passed several parts of the Women's Health Equity Act, including funding for screening tests for breast cancer. The government also now requires new health studies to include women as subjects rather than assume that research on men applies to women.

In 1991 Dr. Bernadine Healy became the first woman to head the National Institutes of Health.

What advances have women made in the military since 1980?

More than 22,000 new jobs in the different services have opened up to women. Since 1993 women have been allowed to serve as combat pilots and aboard combat ships.

Have women led any important peace demonstrations since 1980?

In 1983, to protest the use of nuclear missiles, women set up a peace camp outside the Seneca Army Depot in upstate New York. About 135 women began a fifteen-mile walk to the camp from Seneca Falls, where the U.S. women's movement started in 1848. But before they reached the camp they were stopped by an angry mob waving U.S. flags. The women sat down in the hope that the mob would quiet down, but the women were immediately arrested—not the people who had threatened them.

About 40,000 women served in the Gulf War in 1991.

Were any women honored as peacemakers in the 1990s?

In 1997 Jody Williams became the third U.S. woman to receive the Nobel Peace Prize. As the coordinator of the

A Plea for Peace

In 1982, after President Ronald Reagan warned of the military threat of the Soviet Union, 11-year-old Samantha Smith wrote to the Soviet prime minister, Yuri Andropov, and urged him not to start a war. Andropov gave a public reply to her letter, reassuring her that he, too, wanted peace, and he invited her to visit the Soviet Union with her family. She went on a trip that made newspaper headlines and continued to speak out for peace after her return. Sadly, however, in 1985 she was killed in a plane crash with her father.

International Campaign to Ban Landmines (ICBL), she helped to draw attention to the horror of these explosive devices, which kill and injure some 26,000 people every year. Williams and ICBL were responsible for getting ninety nations to sign a treaty to end their use of land mines.

What important books have been written about women since 1980?

Hundreds of books on women and their concerns have been published since 1980. Women wrote biographies of such major historical figures as Susan B. Anthony, Eleanor Roosevelt, Sojourner Truth, and Emma Goldman. They also wrote runaway best-sellers on women's issues, such as Deborah F. Tannen's *You Just Don't Understand*, which looks at the different ways in which men and women communicate

A Nobel Prize Winner

In 1993 Toni Morrison became the second U.S. woman and the first African American to win the Nobel Prize in literature. All her books deal with the experiences of African Americans. *Beloved* (1987), for example, is based in part on the real story of Margaret Garner, who escaped from slavery with her children, was tracked down, and then tried to kill her children before they could be recaptured. About her Nobel Prize, Morrison said, "I felt I represented a whole world of women who either were silenced or who had never received the imprimatur of the established literary world."

Designing Memorials

In 1981 Maya Ying Lin, while still an architectural student, won a national contest to design the Vietnam Veterans Memorial in Washington, D.C. In her design huge slabs of polished black granite, set into the landscape, were etched with 58,000 some names of Americans killed in the Vietnam War. Some veterans protested that the design was too abstract and cold, but after the memorial was unveiled in 1982 it became one of the most-visited monuments in the capital and thousands of people left flowers, medals, letters, and the like near the names of loved ones. In 1989 Lin designed another much-visited monument, the Civil Rights Memorial in Atlanta.

their feelings. Some books, such as Susan Faludi's award-winning *Backlash*, examined recent threats to women's rights; others, such Clarissa Pinkola Estés's *Women Who Run with the Wolves*, offered inspiration for women to take chances and explore new approaches to life.

In 1996 the American Library Association gave Judy Blume a lifetime achievement award for her many fictional works about feisty young girls.

Who have been some important fiction writers since 1980?

Alice Walker became the first African American woman to be awarded the Pulitzer Prize in fiction, for *The Color Purple* (1982), later made into a movie. The second African American woman to win this prize was Toni Morrison, who later won the Nobel Prize. Among

The Guerrilla Girls

Formed in 1985, the Guerrilla Girls boldly attacked discrimination against women artists and artists of color. They put up posters on New York City streets that named museums and galleries that did not show women or nonwhite artists' work. Wearing huge gorilla masks, they appeared at demonstrations and public meetings as, in their words, "the conscience of the art world." In an interview in their 1995 book, *Confessions of the Guerrilla Girls*, one member said: "We've made dealers, curators, critics and collectors accountable. And things have actually gotten better for women and artists of color. With lots of backsliding."

the other winners of the Pulitzer Prize in fiction have been Alison Lurie, Anne Tyler, Jane Smiley, E. Annie Proulx, and Carol Shields.

Louise Erdrich became the first Native American woman to earn the National Book Critics Circle Award for Fiction, for *Love Medicine* (1984). Leslie Marmon Silko, a recipient of one of the "genius" awards from the MacArthur Foundation, has been described as "the most accomplished Indian writer of her generation."

Many other women have been hailed as major voices in fiction, including Mary Gordon, with novels from a Catholic woman's point of view; Cynthia Ozick, who writes about Jewish themes; Barbara Kingsolver, with magical tales of ordinary people; Amy Tan, who interweaves the experiences of Chinese immigrant mothers and American-born daughters; Mona Simpson, with insights into family bonds; Gloria Naylor, who portrays strong black women; Joyce Carol Oates, writing in a variety of styles; and Sandra Cisneros, Judith Ortiz Cofer, and Julia Alvarez, who describe the Latina experience.

What honors have women poets and playwrights received since 1980?

In 1992 Mona Van Duyn was the first woman to be named U.S. poet laureate. The next year Rita Dove became the first African American to receive this honor. As an indication of the growing esteem for women poets, Maya Angelou was asked to read one of her poems at the inauguration of President Bill Clinton in 1993.

In 1983 composer Ellen Taaffe Zwillich became the first woman to receive the Pulitzer Prize in music; in 1991 Shulamit Ran became the second woman to receive this award.

A Crossover Dream

In 1993 Selena (Selena Quintanilla Pérez) won a Grammy Award for best Mexican American album. To many young Chicanas, especially in Texas, she was *the* pop music star. Selena dreamed of reaching an even broader audience and recorded an English-language album, *Dreaming of You*. Just before this record was released in 1995, Selena was murdered, so she did not live to see her album soar to the top of the pop charts.

Barbra Streisand, in costume for her starring role in *Yentl*, steps behind the camera to check a scene. She directed, produced, and co-wrote the 1983 film.

During the 1980s three women playwrights won the Pulitzer Prize: Beth Henley, Marsha Norman, and Wendy Wasserstein. In 1996 Anna Deaveare Smith received a "genius" grant from the MacArthur Foundation after writing and performing two highly praised pieces about racism.

In 1980 Sherry Lansing became the first woman president of a major Holly-wood studio, at Twentieth Century Fox.

Have many women directed films since 1980?

In recent years women have made not only inde-pendent films but an increasing number of films for Hollywood studios. One of the best-known women direc-

Women Friends in Films

In addition to films showing strong, independent women, Hollywood has released a number of films portraying the value of women's friendships. In *Thelma & Louise* the exploits of two women "buddies," played by Geena Davis and Susan Sarandon, drew crowds in 1991. In the 1990s *Fried Green Tomatoes, The Joy Luck Club* (based on Amy Tan's novel), *Little Women, How to Make an American Quilt,* and *Waiting to Exhale* all focused on the importance of supportive relationships among women.

tors is Penny Marshall, with such films as *Big, Awakenings,* and *A League of Their Own* to her credit. Another top woman director is actress Barbra Streisand, with such films as *Yentl* and *The Prince of Tides.* Other films by women directors include Amy Heckerling's *Clueless,* Nora Ephron's *Sleepless in Seattle,* and Julie Dash's *Daughters of the Dust.*

What were some Olympics highlights in the 1980s and 1990s?

In 1984 Mary Lou Retton won the first American gold medal in the all-around gymnastics event, helping to popularize the sport in this country. Valerie Brisco-Hooks became the first Olympic runner to win both the 200-meter and 400-meter events, and Joan Benoit won the first women's Olympic marathon.

In 1992 Jackie Joyner-Kersee became the first woman to win gold in the heptathlon in two successive Olympics (she also won a silver in this event in 1984). The heptathlon

In 1992 Kristi Yamaguchi became the first Asian American to win a gold medal in figure skating.

Women Keep Winning

In 1985 Libby Riddles became the first woman to win one of the world's toughest races, the Iditarod Trail dog sled race across 1,100 miles of wilderness in Alaska. She and her dogs covered the distance in 17 days. For the next three years another woman, Susan Butcher, won this annual race, and she won again in 1990. People began wearing T-shirts that said, "Alaska: Where men are men and women win the Iditarod."

Jackie Joyner-Kersee prepares to hurl the javelin in the heptathlon at the World Track Championships in Rome, Italy, in 1987. She won a gold medal in the event, which includes high jump, long jump, triple jump, pole vault, shot put, discus, and javelin competitions.

Stacy Allison was the first American woman to reach the top of the world's tallest mountain, Mount Everest, in 1988.

includes seven events, such as the hurdles and long jump, to indicate best overall track-and-field star.

In 1994 Bonnie Blair won her third straight gold in the 500-meter speed skating event and her second gold in the 1,000-meter event. She was the first woman to win five gold medals in the winter games.

In the 1996 games the U.S. women's teams won gold in gymnastics, basketball, softball, and soccer. Also, swimmer Amy Van Dyken became the first U.S. woman to win four gold medals at one Olympics.

GLOSSARY

A

abolitionist opposed to slavery; also, a person who was active in the movement to end slavery in the United States

abortion ending a pregnancy before a baby is born

American Woman Suffrage Association an organization started in 1869 by Lucy Stone, Julia Ward Howe, and others to fight for women's right to vote; it supported the 15th Amendment

B

bloomers a 19th-century outfit with loose, puffed-out pants topped by a dress that went just below the knees; it was named after Amelia Bloomer

C

cacica Spanish name for a woman chief

Chicana an American female of Mexican descent

clan mother the woman believed to be the common ancestor for a group of people

consciousness-raising (CR) groups small, informal gatherings started by women in the 1960s; participants discussed their personal experiences as a way of increasing their awareness of political and social issues

D

Daughters of Liberty a secret group of women who protested British rule in America during the mid-1700s

domestics women who are hired to do household work

domestic violence physical attacks by one household member on another, most often by a husband on a wife

E

Equal Rights Amendment a proposed constitutional amendment calling for equality of rights for both sexes; it was first put forward in the 1920s, reactivated in the 1940s, and passed by Congress in 1972, but it failed to be approved by enough states to become part of the U.S. Constitution

ERA abbreviation for Equal Rights Amendment

F

feminist a supporter of equal political, economic, and social rights for women

15th Amendment the constitutional amendment, approved in 1870, that gave African American men the right to vote

flappers young women in the 1920s who rebelled against the social standards for ladylike behavior; they often wore short skirts and bobbed (cut short) their hair

G

glass ceiling an invisible barrier of discrimination that keeps women and people of color from gaining the top jobs in many companies

I

indentured servant a person who is required to work for a set number of years for a master but is then given her or his freedom

L

Latina a female of Latin American origin or descent living in the United States

lynching murder, usually by hanging, carried out by a mob; in the United States many African Americans were lynched by white mobs

M

matrilineal tracing ancestry through the women of a society

midwives women who help deliver babies

mutual-aid societies groups in which members contribute to a common fund, which is used as insurance for members in need of money

N

National American Woman Suffrage Association a national suffrage organization, formed in 1890, that united the National Woman Suffrage Association and the American Woman Suffrage Association

National Woman Suffrage Association an organization started in 1869 by Susan B. Anthony and Elizabeth Cady Stanton to fight for women's rights, especially the right to vote; it did not support the 15th Amendment because it wanted an amendment giving all U.S. citizens the right to vote

National Woman's Party a national suffrage group formed in 1916 by Alice Paul and other women; it was considered more radical than the National American Woman Suffrage Association

NAWSA abbreviation for National American Woman Suffrage Association

19th Amendment the constitutional amendment, approved in 1920, that gave women the right to vote

NOW abbreviation for the National Organization for Women, an organization for women's rights founded in 1966 by Betty Friedan and other women

P

pacifist a person who opposes all wars

picture bride a woman chosen for marriage through an exchange of photographs; in American history usually referring to a Japanese bride chosen by a male Japanese immigrant in the early 20th century

Puritans a 16th- and 17th-century group of Protestants who wanted to reform the Church of England and adopted strict moral rules; many came to America to practice their religion freely

Q

Quakers members of the Religious Society of Friends, started in England in the mid-16th century; they do not believe priests are needed and emphasize the "inner light" in each person; they opposed slavery

R

Roe v. Wade a 1973 Supreme Court case in which the Court upheld a woman's right to choose to have an abortion in the first several months of pregnancy

S

sachem a Native American chief

Seneca Falls convention the first women's rights convention in the United States, organized by Elizabeth Cady Stanton, Lucretia Mott, and other women and held in 1848 in Seneca Falls, New York

seminaries secondary schools; in the 19th century these schools provided the equivalent of today's high school education

settlement house a community center, usually in a city, that provides various social services; in the late 19th and early 20th century the social workers often lived in the center

sexual harassment being annoyed repeatedly because of one's gender; it is illegal if it interferes with one's ability to work or creates a very uncomfortable work situation

suffrage the right to vote

suffragist a person who calls for expanding the right to vote, especially the right of women to vote

sweatshop a factory where employees are required to work long hours for low wages in unhealthy surroundings

T

temperance societies groups that called for moderation in or an end to the use of alcoholic beverages

tipi a cone-shaped tent dwelling made by Plains Indian women

Title IX a 1972 federal law that prohibits sex discrimination in any school receiving money from the U.S. government

W

WAVES an abbreviation for Women Accepted for Volunteer Emergency Service, the division of the U.S. Navy in which women served during World War II

women of color nonwhite women, including women of African, Asian, Hispanic, Native American, and Pacific Islander descent

Women's Army Corps the division of the U.S. Army in which women served during World War II; the women enlistees were called WACs

Woman's Christian Temperance Union an organization formed by Protestant women in 1874 with the purpose of stopping or at least reducing the use of alcoholic beverages

women's liberation movement an effort, starting in 1967–68, by radical feminists to free women from perceived abuses of power by men

Women's Trade Union League an organization started in 1903 by working-class, middle-class, and upper-class women with the purpose of gaining better working conditions for women and supporting women strikers

SELECTED
BIBLIOGRAPHY

Allen, Paula Gunn. *The Sacred Hoop: Recovering the Feminine in American Indian Traditions*. Boston: Beacon Press, 1986.

Bataille, Gretchen M., editor. *Native American Women: A Biographical Dictionary*. New York: Garland Publishing, 1993.

Baxandall, Rosalyn, Linda Gordon, and Susan Reverby, editors. *America's Working Women: A Documentary History—1600 to the Present*. New York: Vintage Books, 1976.

Berkinow, Louise, in association with the National Women's History Project. *The American Women's Almanac*. New York: Berkley Books, 1997.

Broude, Norma, and Mary D. Garrard, editors. *The Power of Feminist Art: The American Movement of the 1970s, History and Impact*. New York: Harry N. Abrams, 1994.

Cott, Nancy F., editor. *The Young Oxford History of Women in the United States*, 11 volumes. New York: Oxford University Press, 1994.

Davis, Flora. *Moving the Mountain: The Women's Movement in America Since 1960*. New York: Simon and Schuster, 1991.

De Pauw, Linda Grant. *Founding Mothers: Women of America in the Revolutionary Era*. Boston: Houghton Mifflin, 1975.

Evans, Sara M. *Born for Liberty*. New York: Free Press, 1989.

Flexner, Eleanor. *Century of Struggle: The Woman's Rights Movement in the United States*. Revised edition. Cambridge: Harvard University Press, 1975.

Giddings, Paula. *When and Where I Enter: The Impact of Black Women on Race and Sex in America*. New York: Bantam Books, 1988.

Green, Rayna. *Women in American Indian Society*. New York: Chelsea House, 1992.

Heinemann, Sue. *Timelines of American Women's History*. New York: Perigee, 1996.

Hine, Darlene Clark, Elsa Barkley Brown, and Rosalyn Terborg-Penn, editors. *Black Women in America: An Historical Encyclopedia*, 2 volumes. Bloomington: Indiana University Press, 1994.

Holm, Jeanne. *Women in the Military: An Unfinished Revolution.* Revised edition. Novato, CA: Presidio, 1992.

James, Edward T., with Janet Wilson James and Paul S. Boyer. *Notable American Women 1607–1950: A Biographical Dictionary*, 3 volumes. Cambridge: Harvard University Press, 1971.

Kass-Simon, G., and Patricia Farnes, editors. *Women of Science: Righting the Record.* Bloomington: Indiana University Press, 1993.

Kerber, Linda K., and Jane Sherron de Hart, editors. *Women's America: Refocusing the Past.* Third edition. New York: Oxford University Press, 1991.

Lerner, Gerda. *The Female Experience: An American Documentary.* Indianapolis: Bobbs-Merrill, 1977.

———. editor. *Black Women in White America: A Documentary History.* New York: Vintage Books, 1973.

Levine, Suzanne, and Harriet Lyons, editors. *The Decade of Women: A Ms. History of the Seventies in Words and Pictures.* New York: Paragon, 1980.

Luchetti, Cathy, in collaboration with Carol Olwell. *Women of the West.* St. George, UT: Antelope Island Press, 1982.

Lunardini, Christine. *What Every Woman Should Know about Women's History: 200 Events That Shaped Our Destiny.* Holbrook, MA: Bob Adams, 1994.

Moynihan, Ruth Barnes, Cynthia Ussett, and Laurie Crumpacker. *Second to None: A Documentary History of American Women*, 2 volumes. Lincoln: University of Nebraska Press, 1993.

Nakono, Mei. *Japanese American Women: Three Generations, 1890–1990.* San Francisco: Mina Press and the National Japanese American Historical Society, 1990.

National Women's History Project. "Las Mujeres: Mexican American/Chicana Women." Windsor, CA: National Women's History Project.

Papachristou, Judith. *Women Together: A History in Documents of the Women's Movement in the United States.* New York: Alfred A. Knopf, 1976.

Peavy, Linda, and Ursula Smith. *Pioneer Women: The Lives of Women on the Frontier.* New York: Smithmark Publishers, 1996.

Read, Phyllis J., and Bernard L. Witlieb. *The Book of Women's Firsts.* New York: Random House, 1992.

Ruether, Rosemary Radford, and Rosemary Skinner Keller, editors. *Women and Religion in America*, 3 volumes. San Francisco: Harper and Row, 1981–86.

Schlissel, Lillian. *Women's Diaries of the Westward Journey.* New York: Schocken Books, 1982.

Sherr, Lynn, and Jurate Kazickas. *Susan B. Anthony Slept Here: A Guide to American Women's Landmarks.* New York: Times Books, 1994.

Sicherman, Barbara, and Carol Hurd Green, with Ilene Kantrov and Harriette Walker, editors. *Notable American Women: The Modern Period.* Cambridge: Harvard University Press, 1980.

Smith, Jessie Carney, editor. *Epic Lives: One Hundred Black Women Who Made a Difference.* Detroit: Visible Ink Press, 1993.

Solomon, Barbara Miller. *In the Company of Educated Women.* New Haven: Yale University Press, 1985.

Telgen, Diane, and Jim Kamp, editors. *Notable Hispanic Women.* Detroit: Gale Research, 1993.

Vare, Ehtlie Ann, and Greg Ptacek, *Mothers of Invention: From the Bra to the Bomb, Forgotten Women and Their Incredible Ideas.* New York: William Morrow, 1987.

Weatherford, Doris. *American Women's History: An A to Z of People, Organizations, Issues, and Events.* New York: Prentice-Hall, 1994.

Weiser, Marjorie P. I., and Jean S. Arbeiter. *Womanlist.* New York : Atheneum, 1981.

Wertheimer, Barbara Meyer. *We Were There: The Story of Working Women in America.* New York: Pantheon Books, 1977.

Woloch, Nancy. *Women and the American Experience.* New York: Alfred A. Knopf, 1984.

Yung, Judy. *Chinese Women of America.* Seattle: University of Washington Press, 1986.

THE NEW YORK PUBLIC LIBRARY'S
RECOMMENDED READING LIST

Archer, Jules. *Breaking Barriers: The Feminist Revolution, from Susan B. Anthony to Margaret Sanger to Betty Friedan.* New York: Viking, 1991

Bundles, A'Leila Perry. *Madam C. J. Walker.* New York: Chelsea House Publishers, 1991

Chang, Ina. *A Separate Battle: Women and the Civil War.* New York: Lodestar Books, 1991

Colman, Penny. *A Woman Unafraid: The Achievements of Frances Perkins.* New York: Atheneum, 1993

Cullen-Dupont, Kathryn. *Elizabeth Cady Stanton and Women's Liberty.* New York: Facts on File, 1992

Delany, Sarah and A. Elizabeth Delany with Amy Hill Hearth. *Having Our Say: The Delany Sisters' First 100 Years.* New York: Kodansha International, 1993

Ferris, Jeri. *Native American Doctor: The Story of Susan LaFlesche Picotte.* Minneapolis: Carolrhoda Books, Inc., 1991

Fireside, Bryna J. *Is There a Woman in the House...or Senate?* Morton Grove, IL: Albert Whitman & Co., 1994

Freedman, Russell. *Eleanor Roosevelt: a Life of Discovery.* New York: Clarion Books, 1993

Garza, Hedda. *Barred from the Bar: A History of Women in the Legal Profession.* New York: Watts, 1996

Goldston, Sydele E. *Changing Woman of the Apache.* New York: Franklin Watts, 1996

Harrington, Geri. *Jackie Joyner-Kersee: Champion Athlete.* New York: Chelsea House, 1995

Holden, Henry M. with Lori Griffith *Ladybirds: The Untold Story of Women Pilots in America.* Freedom, NJ: Black Hawk Pub. Co., 1993

Jeffrey, Laura S. *Barbara Jordan: Congresswoman, Lawyer, Educator.*
Springfield, NJ: Enslow, 1997

Keller, Evelyn Fox. *A Feeling for the Organism: The Life and Work
of Barbara McClintock.* New York: W.H. Freeman and Co., 1983

Kleinbaum, Nancy H. *The Magnificent Seven: The Authorized Story
of American Gold.* New York: Bantam, 1996

Kraft, Betsy Harvey. *Mother Jones: One Woman's Fight for Labor.*
New York: Clarion Books, 1995

McKissack, Patricia C. and Fredrick. *Sojourner Truth: Ain't I a Woman?*
New York: Scholastic, 1992

Macy, Sue. *Winning Ways: A Photohistory of American Women in Sports.*
New York: Henry Holt and Co., 1996

Margolies-Mezvinsky, Marjorie with Barbara Feinman. *A Woman's Place...
The Freshmen Women Who Changed the Face of Congress.* New York:
Crown Publishers, 1994

Nichols, Joan Kane. *A Matter of Conscience: The Trial of Anne Hutchinson.*
Austin, TX: Raintree Steck-Vaughn, 1993

Parks, Rosa. *Quiet Strength.* Grand Rapids, MI: Zondervan Publishing
House, 1994

Peavy, Linda and Ursula Smith. *Pioneer Women: The Lives of American
Women on the Frontier.* New York: Smithmark, 1996

Savage, Candace. *Cowgirls.* Berkeley, CA: Ten Speed Press, 1996

Sheafer, Silvia Anne. *Women in America's Wars.* Springfield, NJ:
Enslow, 1996

Siegel, Beatrice. *Marian Wright Edelman: The Making of a Crusader.*
New York: Simon and Schuster Books for Young Readers, 1995

Veglahn, Nancy J. *Women Scientists.* New York: Facts On File, 1991

Wheeler, Leslie A. *Rachel Carson.* Englewood Cliffs, NJ: Silver Burdett
Press, 1991

Whitney, Sharon. *The Equal Rights Amendment: The History and the
Movement.* New York: Watts, 1984

Zeinert, Karen. *Those Remarkable Women of the American Revolution.*
Brookfield, CT: Millbrook Press, 1996

INDEX

I
ice skating, 169, 170
Idaho, 76, 78
Idár, Jovita, 99
Iditarod (dog sled race), 169
Illinois, 61-62, 83, 100, 157
Illinois Women's Alliance, 82
immigrants
    Asian restrictions, 103, 104
    settlement houses, 85
    working conditions,
        58-59, 80-81, 83
    See also specific groups
indentured servants, 11, 173
Indianapolis 500
    (auto race), 154
Indiana University, 53
Indian Territory, 52, 67, 74, 94
Institute for Colored Youth
    (Phila.), 54
International Campaign to
    Ban Landmines, 165
international politics, 104,
    118, 125
International Typographical
    Union, 60
International Women's Year,
    143
inventions and patents, 18,
    83, 94
Irish immigrants, 58-59, 80-81
Iroquois people, 8, 9, 10, 22-23
Italian immigrants, 80

J
Jack, Ellen E., 74
Jackson, Helen Hunt, 74
Jacobi, Mary Putnam, 93
Jacobs, Harriet, 40
James, Sarah, 160
James, William, 91
Jamestown colony, 9-11
Japanese Americans, 129,
    130, 131, 138
    picture brides, 104, 173
jazz, 120
Jemison, Alice, 119
Jemison, Mae, 163
Jemison, Mary, 17
Jewett, Sarah Orne, 96
Jewish women
    garment workers, 108
    organizations, 84, 86, 89,
        104
    rabbis, 147

Johnson, Georgia Douglass,
    118
Jones, Margo, 132
Jones, Mother (Mary Harris
    Jones), 107
Jones, Sissieretta, 94
Jordan, Barbara, 143
journalism. *See* press
Joyner-Kersee, Jackie, 169,
    170
judges, 116, 125, 126, 155
jury duty, 48, 127-28, 143

K
Kaahumanu, 31
Kansas, 75, 76, 77, 87, 100,
    158
Kassebaum, Nancy, 156
Kearney, Belle, 99
Keene, Carolyn (pseud.), 127
Keene, Laura, 63
Keller, Helen, 90
Kelley, Florence, 83, 85
Kennedy, John F., 137
Kentucky, 109, 158
Kepley, Ada H., 61
Key, Eliabeth, 15-16
King, Billie Jean, 154
King, Coretta Scott, 140, 145
King, Martin Luther, Jr., 134,
    136, 140
King Philip's War, 16, 17
Kingsolver, Barbara, 167
Kingston, Maxine Hong, 152
Kirkpatrick, Jeane, 155
Klondike, 74
Knight, Margaret, 94
Knight, Sarah Kemble, 18
Knights of Labor, 82
Kong Tai Heong, 92
Kreps, Juanita, 143
Ku Klux Klan, 79
Kunin, Madeleine, 158

L
labor movement
    Chicana activists, 144
    Equal Rights Amendment
        opponents, 128
    equal rights laws, 144, 145
    19th-century, 58, 59, 60, 82
    early 1900s, *106*, 107-9,
        174
    1930s, 122-24
    1960s-70s, 144-45

woman suffrage group, 98-
    99
Women's Trade Union
    League, 107, 108, 174
work days and hours, 58,
    81, 83, 107
    See also pay; strikes
Ladies' Magazine, 55
Ladies Professional Golf
    Association, 132
La Flesche, Rosalie, 72
La Flesche, Susan (later
    Picotte), 94
La Flesche, Susette (later
    Tibbles), 72
Lamont, Blanche, *53*
Laney, Lucy Craft, 91
Lange, Dorothea, 122
Lange, Mother Mary Elizabeth
    (Elizabeth Clovis Lange),
    50
Lansing, Sherry, 168
Latinas, 71-72, 156, 163, 164,
    167, 173 (*see also* Chicanas;
    Puerto Rican women)
law
    abortion legalization, 149
    segregation challenges, 70,
        130-31, 134
    sexual harassment ruling,
        161
    slavery challenges, 15-16,
        22
    woman suffrage chal-
        lenges, 77
    women judges, 116, 125,
        126, 155
    women's protective, 83-84,
        116, 117, 125, 128, 137,
        159, 164
    women's rights, 48, 133,
        142, 145, 147
    See also specific laws
lawyers, 61-62, 117
Lazarus, Emma, 96
League of Mexican Feminists,
    The, 99
League of United Latin
    Citizens, 126
League of Women Voters,
    116, 117
Leavitt, Henrietta, 112
Lee, Ann (Mother Lee), 27
Lee, Rebecca (later
    Crumpler), 61

Photography Credits

Pages 14, 21, 23, 26, 31, 36, 43, 46, 50, 51, 56, 57, 68, 75, 78, 81, 82, 93, 98, 105, and 106, the Picture Collection of The New York Public Library, Astor, Lenox and Tilden Foundations; pages 33, 80, 124, 130, and 137, the Photographs and Prints Division, The Schomburg Center for Research in Black Culture, The New York Public Library, Astor, Lenox and Tilden Foundations; page 8, Rare Books and Manuscripts Department, New York Public Library, the Astor, Lenox and Tilden Foundations; pages 10, 39, 42, 53, 58, 85, 87, 110, 121, 122, 130, courtesy the Library of Congress; page 100, Corbis-Bettman; pages 135, 138, 154, and 170, UPI/Corbis-Bettman; page 95, courtesy of the National Baseball Library, Cooperstown, NY; page 151, courtesy the U.S. Department of Defense; page 160, Sue Heinemann; page 163, courtesy of NASA.